WHAT PEOPLE ARE SAYING ABOUT PROJECT OTY AND *TRANSFORM WITH CONFIDENCE*

"I learned what kind of a person I want to be."

"It helped me think about what I really need to do to succeed in my future."

"It helped me realize what I need to do to work at a job I love."

"It helped me organize my thoughts and I learned a lot about myself."

"It helped open up my eyes to what is possible in the future."

"It made me think about what I want to do with my life."

"It made me think a lot about my goals and priorities."

"It helped me figure out some of my unique strengths."

"It made me realize how to make my goals more attainable."

"It helped me see how to deal with disappointments in life."

"It helped me see how I could accomplish a 10-year plan."

"It opened my mind about my strengths and how I can use them to succeed."

"It helped me realize what I really want for my future."

"It made me think about what I can do right now that will help me work towards my future vision."

"Relevant, engaging and a delightful recipe for cooking up long-term personal success."

"This is applicable for anyone at any age."

"I loved how easy the content is to absorb but still makes you think."

"Right out of the gate, *Transform with Confidence* will light a fire under your butt and energize you to go make a difference in your life."

"This book allowed me to learn things about myself that I never slowed down in my busy life to analyze. I was able to identify my path to reaching my ultimate self."

Transform with Confidence

Create YOUR World

JEFF OTIS

Copyright © 2017 by Jeff Otis

All rights reserved. This book or any portion thereof may not be reproduced or used in any manner whatsoever without the express written permission of the publisher except for the use of brief quotations in a book review.

Printed in the United States of America

First Printing, 2017

Design by Indigo: Editing, Design, and More

ISBN 978-0-692-14524-1

Project OTY Publications
Beaverton, Oregon

www.ProjectOTY.com

CONTENTS

Special Thanks vii
Introduction 3

Part One: The Process
Chapter One: Transformation and Life 13
Chapter Two: Unique Strengths 27
Chapter Three: Your Vision 37
Chapter Four: Ego, Fears and Motivations 51
Chapter Five: Crystalizing Your Vision 71
Chapter Six: Enrolling Others 83
Chapter Seven: Goals 95
Chapter Eight: Steps 107

Part Two: Lessons
Chapter Nine: Accountable or Victim 119
Chapter Ten: You Choose Your "Accident" 133
Chapter Eleven: Practice and Focus 149
Chapter Twelve: Appreciating the Moment 161
Chapter Thirteen: Leadership and Confidence 171
Chapter Fourteen: Gratitude and Peace 183

Epilogue: Dream Big! 191
Who's Jeff Otis? 193

SPECIAL THANKS

What I love about creating this book and the idea of creating the World that YOU want to live in is that so many other people just want to live in that same world. A world that is peaceful, thoughtful, grateful, happy and safe.

When I started the journey of building Project OTY and the writing of *Transform with Confidence*, I found that the right person after the right person kept coming into my world.

I am grateful for the people that have come into my life and I owe a special thanks to many people for helping me in the pursuit of bringing this book to a reality.

Thank you Sammy. Stay Amazing! Thank you Betsy. Your feedback and instincts are brilliant. Thank you Cindi. You're an Angel. Thank you Cheryl for believing. Thank you to Mike and the Meingast for the learning opportunities. They were unbelievable.

Thank you to the countless coaches, teammates, golf buddies, co-workers, family and friends. You are what make life fun. And a special thanks to Suzanne for your enlightenment, unique strengths and your words of wisdom. What an amazing journey.

Enjoy the Book!

"The MEANING OF LIFE is to find your gift.

The PURPOSE OF LIFE is to give it away."
~ Pablo Picasso

INTRODUCTION

No two people are the same. Everyone has experienced a unique series of moments and influences that have affected them and led them to be who they are, do what they do and believe what they believe. No two people have had the same parents, teachers, coaches, friends, bosses or experiences, but <u>everyone</u> has encountered a challenge at one time or another. I have dubbed life's big, life-altering challenges, "Transformative Moments."

In addition to the Transformative Moments (good and bad) that most of us experience, such as falling in love or dealing with an illness, we are now being exposed through the internet to information that is often transformative in nature. And, not only do we have 24/7 access to the constant drama of the news, but we are also being overwhelmed with manufactured depictions of success and happiness that often contradict the definitions of success that have been impressed upon us from an early age by our families and communities.

Perhaps you are seventeen today, or twenty-seven, thirty-seven, forty-seven or even fifty-seven. The fact is, no matter what your age, we are all going through a transformative time unlike anything we've ever experienced before in the history of the world. As a consequence, many of us are often confused by the many competing definitions of success being pushed on us and often unsure of how to create the lives we want to live. We are all managing personal Transformative Moments while simultaneously navigating and processing the onslaught of information, expectations and images we are being exposed to on a daily basis through our modern media.

The current pace of life is difficult for many of us and can be particularly difficult for our young adults and growing kids. As a result, we are seeing ever-increasing levels of anxiety among the entire population, with particularly high levels in the teen population. In fact, prescriptions being written for teen anxiety are increasing at an alarming rate. The parents and grandparents of today's kids did not grow up in the same world these kids are now inhabiting. It's all new.

Our current educational system is not equipped to teach us how to navigate Transformative Moments, much less this Transformative Era. The result of this lack of guidance is that when faced with Transformative Moments, many of us fall victim to counter-productive behaviors that lead us to blame others or remain passive. Without a clear and authentic personal Vision or way to achieve it, it is less likely that we will have the confidence to adopt accountable behaviors that will lead us to reinvent ourselves and our world.

Over the course of my career, in order to address and potentially resolve the many issues we humans are facing both personally and collectively, I have continued to ask myself the following questions:

- How do we empower ourselves and others to manage the onslaught of information hitting all of us?
- How do we empower ourselves and others to manage what we perceive to be Transformative Moments?
- How can we create a path that caters to individualized learning in an educational structure that values conformity?
- And...how do we empower ourselves and others to be personally accountable for our choices in life, so that we all have the opportunity to create the lives we truly want?

If we can answer these questions, we can reverse the trajectory we are currently on and create a sustainable culture of accountability in which we all have the opportunity to solve some of the world's biggest problems. By becoming aware of and utilizing our Unique Strengths in concert with the Unique Strengths of others in order to create and achieve our highest Vision, we share our best selves with our communities and the world at large. By sharing our gifts, we empower those around us to do the same. In essence, we are "paying it forward" by enlisting the engagement of others in our quest for self-realization. This is how "personal accountability" becomes the catalyst for positive change!

Project OTY (Outstanding, Talented You) and *Transform with Confidence*

After fifteen years in the employment staffing industry and ten years in the online marketing, messaging and advertising world, I have spent many hours working with thousands of people. I have listened to their concerns, fears and insecurities, as well as their dreams and visions for their futures. My expertise in the areas of sales, marketing, messaging and leadership, in addition to my interest in human behavior, neuroscience and neuromarketing have led me to the insights I am happy to be sharing with you in this book.

My unique experiences, moments and influences have led me to pursue my particular Vision, which is and has been to create the curriculum for an online program I call Project OTY (Outstanding, Talented You). *Transform*

Introduction

with Confidence is meant to serve as the companion book for Project OTY and provides a more thorough explanation of the concepts underlying the Project OTY curriculum. Both this book and the online program will introduce you to a process for identifying and achieving your unique Vision.

Around 2005, I conceived of and began creating Project OTY with the idea in mind that personal accountability could be promoted by teaching people how to establish the Goals and take the Steps that would lead them to achieve a unique personal Vision, while successfully navigating their own Transformative Moments, as well as this ongoing transformative period in our history.

I have always been fascinated with process, and why people do what they do. I have always wondered why some people live successful, adventurous lives, and some people experience very circumscribed lives dictated by fear. I have been curious about why fear is so prominent in the world and how it manifests itself in so many of our daily situations and interactions. I have also wondered why we have not progressed more as a society and as a world, and why there are times when we encounter so much difficulty living harmoniously with one another.

Project OTY and *Transform with Confidence* both offer an easy-to-follow process created to help those who are interested in identifying and developing their own personal roadmap for success. Students of Project OTY and readers of *Transform with Confidence* are taught how to achieve their Visions by identifying, developing and utilizing their Unique Strengths, managing their fears and learning to navigate Transformative Moments. The process I introduce in the online program as well as in this book is meant to inspire accountable behaviors which ultimately empower students and readers alike to have the confidence to enlist the assistance of others in pursuit of their smaller Goals and larger Visions.

This book is intentionally designed to support the Project OTY effort and share deeper insights about what it means to Transform with Confidence. By working with thousands of people, I have learned that most everybody wants the same things: to feel safe, peaceful and happy. Most of us want to solve our own problems, be able to ask for help from others, and in turn help others solve their problems, but we're often blind to how others may be able to help us, as well as how we might be of assistance to them. My hope is that this book and Project OTY will bridge that gap and empower students and readers with the tools to Transform with Confidence as they encounter life's Transformative Moments.

I've seen the exercises and concepts shared in this book change lives. I've seen people achieve Goals and realize Visions they never imagined possible. We are continually

INTRODUCTION

growing and learning and transforming. Every day we transform a little bit in one way or another. If we are going to consistently Transform, let's make sure that we are doing it with Confidence!

Part One

THE PROCESS

"Every moment of life is precious.

Enjoy each moment, for it's a gift."

~ John Otis

Chapter One

TRANSFORMATION AND LIFE

How to Recognize Transformative Moments

WHAT IS A TRANSFORMATIVE MOMENT?
Throughout our lives we face a variety of moments, influences and events that shape how we experience our lives, how we think about ourselves, what we believe, and the choices we make. Each of us is uniquely affected by our own combination of moments, experiences, and information, and some of these moments are "Transformative Moments." These are the big moments, moments that are over in an instant as well as extended moments that can last for a period of time: puberty, first kiss, graduating from high school, going to college, getting married, getting divorced, landing a job, getting fired, having children, experiencing the death of a loved one, retiring, dealing with illness or injury, and so on. These big moments radically influence our choices and ultimately the direction our lives take.

In addition to experiencing our own unique and personal Transformative Moments, we are now experiencing a period in history, due in large part to the speed of technological change, which is an extended or ongoing Transformative Moment. The internet has increased our visibility and our access to the entire world, and it has opened up our ability to connect and communicate like never before. As a result of this, every Tweet, Facebook post, Instagram share or email response feels potentially monumental.

The images, thoughts and reactions you post now will be forever attributed to you, and will stand in as a representation of who you are and what you believe in, regardless of whether you change your mind or grow out of the views you once held. The good news is that you're not alone. Everyone who posts online is now aware that his or her actions online can be scrutinized and judged forever. We're learning that it's a game, and that we must pay particular attention to the persona we create for ourselves and the perceptions we create for others.

As a result, when we go online to connect to our social world through Facebook, Instagram, Twitter, or whatever is the latest forum for self-expression and social interaction, we are now encountering the airbrushed and curated images posted by friends and celebrities, which represent what success and happiness supposedly look like. This new standard for success is set at an unreasonably high level, making it almost impossible to achieve the life we see depicted on our screens every day. Simultaneously, we are being exposed to unending news stories depicting violence and destruction. If a train blows up in Brussels, or a mass shooting occurs in California, we know about it instantly. Young kids, along with the rest of us, are now being tasked with navigating this sort of information on a daily basis.

However, in spite of our advanced technology, our core survival instincts as humans have not changed. The need to feel safe is one of our most basic instincts, so it seems that the onslaught of contradictory images and information is reinforcing a level of stress this world has never experienced before. We are also feeling significantly more empathy, awareness, isolation, connection, fear, anger, hope, and curiosity than at any point in our history. The impact this is having on all human beings is that every decision is now starting to feel like a life-altering proposition. As a result, it seems that many people are living in some state of fear—fear of being wrong, fear of making mistakes, fear of being different, fear of not being good enough, fear of loss, fear of rejection, fear of failure...the list goes on and on...

In the United States, doctors are now writing prescriptions and treating depression and anxiety at an ever-increasing rate. Treating these issues cost the United States over $40 billion dollars a year, and over 70% of countries around the world are reporting a significant increase in their population's anxiety levels (according to the Anxiety and Depression Association of America and JWT Intelligence). Many organizations study these trends with the express purpose of providing their findings to commercial companies so that these companies can better capitalize on consumers' anxieties and fears.

We are also deeply influenced by the messages being disseminated by our governments, leaders, big businesses, and religious and educational institutions. Many of these messages have been designed to put us in boxes and lead us to believe whatever serves the best interest of the entity or organization spreading the information. We humans are simply easier to control and manipulate when we are put in boxes. The trouble with this is that many of these messages prey on our fears and are actually promoting fear-based or victim-based decision making. Without a problem to solve, there is no solution to sell, right? Marketers and messengers go to great lengths to understand what fears they need to speak to in order to motivate individuals in one direction or another.

Society is currently facing two divergent paths—the path of fear and isolation, which leads us to feel like victims without agency over our choices, or the path of self-awareness, growth, and connection, which requires us to be accountable for the choices we make and thereby empowered to create the lives we want. Unfortunately, neither our media nor modern society promotes self-awareness, self-actualization, or personal accountability. This can make it difficult for an individual to set a meaningful life course that will result in a lasting sense of satisfaction and contentment.

We are facing a crisis if we and the generations to come do not learn how to navigate personal Transformative Moments, as well as the constantly transforming environment in which we now live. Although our current educational system does many great things, it does not teach the fundamental skills necessary for self-actualization. Nowhere are we taught how to navigate Transformative Moments or succeed in this Transformative Age. When we are hit by a Transformative Moment, we can either choose to succumb to fear and become a victim of that moment, or choose to learn and grow by assuming personal accountability for that moment.

Some would argue that it is just a part of life to have to "figure it out," or that it is the role of our parents to teach us how to navigate these moments, but the reality is that most everyone you will ever meet is simply limited by his or her own personal experiences and influences. To transform with confidence, we need a process that guides us to use what is unique in each of us in order to move toward our heart-felt dreams, or what I am calling our Visions.

It's easy to be a victim. It's easy to give up, to go along to get along, to refuse to make a choice or a decision, or to hold someone else responsible for how your life is unfolding. It's difficult to be accountable. Imagine what life would be like if we took personal accountability for how we react to Transformative Moments. This book outlines and explains a process that will teach you how to be personally accountable for your decisions, attitudes, and behaviors, and formulate and achieve a Vision that is authentic to you.

A Personal Transformative Moment

I was a successful baseball pitcher all through little league and high school. In high school, my teammates and I won the Oregon State Championship and then I went to Oregon State University on a full scholarship. I had a good freshman year and a really good sophomore year. In fact I was voted a "Top Ten Player" in the United States. As you can imagine, I was really excited going into my junior year. Traditionally, we took a spring trip down south to play teams like Sacramento State, Chico State and UC Riverside. This particular year our first stop was Fresno State.

I was playing the first game of the season on a balmy Friday night. Standing on the mound under the lights feeling strong and confident, I could see the crowd of about five thousand people sitting expectantly in the stands. I loved competing, being in front of a crowd, and being in control of the game. The first batter came to bat, and I felt the butterflies in my stomach I always felt before the first pitch. I repeated my mantra, "I'm throwing strikes today...I'm throwing strikes today..."

As a pitcher you really have to pay attention to the hitters stepping up to bat. You look for little weaknesses or tells, or a look in their eyes that signals what kind of pitch they think you'll throw. In this particular game, the first pitch was a ball, the second pitch was a strike, and the third pitch was a disaster. I felt my right shoulder and elbow pop, and instantly knew something was very wrong. I felt a pain like I'd never felt before.

My injury turned out to be a partial tear of the rotator cuff, so I ended up sitting out that entire year. I literally could not reach my hand up to wash my hair, or pull my shirt off my back without using the other arm. I was twenty at that time, and for twelve years, from the age of eight, I'd literally thrown thousands and thousands of pitches. I probably threw more than any kid would today because since that time, "pitch counts" have been instituted to protect pitchers from throwing out their arms.

Even though I sat out that year, I practiced with the team every day. I taught myself to play catch left-handed just to stay around the baseball field. It took almost twelve months before I started throwing again with my right arm. During that recovery year, I'd watch the games and see professional scouts around the field assessing some of the players on our team for the upcoming baseball draft.

I remember thinking, "I wish they were here watching me today." It had been my Vision from a very early age to play professional baseball. With some anxiety, I also remember thinking, "If I'm not playing baseball after college, what am I going to do? I'm going to have to get a job. What kind of job? What do I want to do? What's somebody going to hire me for?"

I played the following year, but my arm was still really sore. If I played "long toss" for an hour before a game, I could get my arm warmed up enough to pitch. But I always experienced excruciating pain afterwards. Nevertheless, I had a really good year, but I knew I was done, and I knew at that point that I had to start thinking about doing something other than playing professional baseball.

A Transformative Moment on a Global Scale

While driving to work through the peaceful streets of suburban Portland, Oregon, I heard on the radio that a plane had hit one of the World Trade Center towers. I pictured a small prop plane hitting a big building. Ten minutes later, I arrived at work and was immediately confronted by employees asking me if I'd heard or seen what was happening? Of course I hadn't seen anything, so we turned on the TV. The images were shocking yet strangely surreal. For years, the coverage of that event has been in our faces. Terrorist threats and the accompanying fear has become a part of our daily lives. Access to the internet has given us a front row seat to these world events. We can't escape. I remember looking at my daughter and her friends a few years after 9/11, and wondering how they were managing all of this information along with the increased threat of domestic and international terrorism. I clearly remember the questions my daughter and her friends were asking, questions I never even considered when I was their age.

Most of what they were witnessing and reading about didn't make sense to them, just like most of it doesn't make sense to any of us. When we are faced with situations we cannot understand, we tend to create fear-based explanations and become more judgmental, critical, desensitized, and anxious. None of us wants to live like that.

TRANSFORMATIVE TIMES
One Friday night, my daughter had a few friends over for pizza before they walked to the high school for the football game. After the game, the girls came back to

the house, made popcorn, watched movies, and giggled madly until they crashed in their sleeping bags in the family room (after making sure their phones were plugged in to charge overnight, of course). The next morning, after they were all awake, I walked into the family room to ask them if they were ready for breakfast. Each one of these girls was on her phone, checking messages, texts, posts, and news alerts, so anxious at the idea of having missed something!

I clearly recall the anxiety I felt for my daughter as I watched her during those high school years. She was living in a world in which she was having to navigate her online social life while managing her self-image through the lens of social media. She was dealing with this in addition to participating in all her other required and elective activities. She was involved in an online world that nobody had ever taught her how to negotiate. I would listen to her and her friends worry about what so-and-so was thinking or saying or posting online about them. Their connections were so widespread that they were constantly trying to figure out how to deal with competing invitations and social obligations, while simultaneously attempting to define and manage their personas.

This experience my daughter and all of us are now having is obviously not a moment, it's a series of moments that create an ongoing low-level of continual stress. In this

Transformative Age, we are now navigating our social and professional lives through the internet, and for better or worse, it is having a huge impact on our decision-making abilities and our level of inner peace.

Some of us are adapting, but most of us could use some degree of support around how to identify our priorities and focus our attention on what we truly want out of our lives. It is exceedingly challenging to transform with confidence when our attention is constantly being pulled in a million different directions. The program I'm sharing with you in the pages of this book will provide you with the tools to negotiate individual Transformative Moments as well as the demands of living in this Transformative Age.

Recognizing Transformative Moments

How can we recognize Transformative Moments in our own lives, whether the moment is a particular incident, or generalized social pressure to make decisions that may not be motivated by an authentic internal desire? Transformative Moments bring up a lot of questions. *What am I going to be doing? How is this going to affect me? What am I going to lose? What's my life going to look like if I don't fix this problem? What are people going to think of me? What if I look bad? What if I fail? What if I make a bad decision? What if I disappoint my parents? What if my friends don't like me anymore?* All these questions revolve around the fundamental issue of whether or not you will be safe going forward.

It is important to be able to recognize what you define as simply "a moment," as opposed to what you define as a "Transformative Moment." You've got to ask yourself, "Why am I defining this moment to be any bigger than or less than any other moment?" A Transformative Moment isn't always life-altering, although it often is. We experience significant moments all the time, but when a really big moment comes along, it's going to raise questions that may reflect our fears. *How am I going to deal with this moment? Am I prepared for what's beyond this moment? Am I ready to go beyond this moment?*

EXPLANATION OF EXERCISES

In each section of this book, we are going to wrap up the chapter with an exercise. The choice to complete the exercises is completely up to you. However, the information contained in each chapter and exercise is designed to build on the previous chapters and exercises. I encourage you to take the time to do the exercises; they will illuminate the points I'm making in each chapter and move you along with the process as it unfolds.

EXERCISE
IDENTIFYING TRANSFORMATIVE MOMENTS

Briefly write down and describe five Transformative Moments that have had a significant impact on your life.

"Become the most positive and enthusiastic person you know."
~ H. Jackson Brown, Jr.

CHAPTER TWO

UNIQUE STRENGTHS

How to Optimize Your Super Power!

WHAT IS YOUR UNIQUE STRENGTH?

Everyone has strengths and limitations. We are generally aware of our limitations, but are often unaware of our strengths, particularly our special or "Unique Strengths." Everyone has a "Unique Strength." This is your greatest strength, above all other strengths. It has evolved from your unique personality as well as your inborn inclinations and talents, and has been formed and shaped by your experiences, which are comprised of all your unique moments and influences. It's the strength that makes you feel good, the strength that others admire in you. It's your unique gift, your unique ability, your unique quality, your super power!

For the sake of clarity, let me explain that your Unique Strength and your particular talent, skill, or attribute may be one and the same. For instance, you may be able to do something that is traditionally thought of as a talent, like sing beautifully, or learn foreign languages with ease, or dunk a basketball, or draw realistic portraits. And you may very well consider that special talent to be your Unique Strength. Or you may have some ability or quality that is not generally thought of as a "talent," such as being able to ask really good incisive questions, or recognize and appreciate beauty, or empathize with and comfort others. If you have this sort of ability, and you feel this ability gives you a kind of super power, then you may want to consider it to be your Unique Strength, or one of your Unique Strengths.

Think about how you spend your day and how you relate to your family, friends, teachers and even your pets. If you have a dog you take for regular walks, perhaps one of your Unique Strengths is that you are good with animals. If you find that your friends are always asking for your advice about their emotional issues, you could say that one of your Unique Strengths is that you are a good counselor or listener.

The point is that your "Unique Strength" is something—anything—you enjoy doing, that gives you a feeling of confidence, pride, purpose, and power when you are doing it. It is also the attribute/skill/talent/ability other people recognize in you that you may or may not have recognized in yourself. You might be an engaging storyteller, or a really loyal friend. You might have the ability to do complex mathematics. You might be highly organized, or able to recognize the talents and abilities in others. The list is endless!

The good news is that you can have more than one Unique Strength, nonetheless there is usually one that stands out. Your strengths will grow and evolve over time as you do. You may feel that your ability at sports is one of your Unique Strengths when you are younger, the way I did, but may find that strength dropping away over time as another takes its place. There is also the probability that one of the Unique Strengths you identified when you were younger will become more developed or may even morph into an entirely different strength as you grow and change. For instance, when I stopped playing baseball and entered into a career in sales and marketing, I developed a Unique Strength that enabled me to identify and deeply understand the motivations behind why people behave the way they do, and then tailor strategies to help them achieve what they did not think was possible.

Even though I would not have been able to identify these Unique Strengths when I was playing baseball in college, I was later able to see how the discipline of practicing a sport seriously, and the team work required to be successful, were essential in developing the abilities I am now using to create and teach the strategies I'm outlining in this book. In other words, nothing you do, pursue, or experience, ever goes to waste. All the moments and experiences you have during your life, combined with your desire to continue learning, contribute to the ongoing evolution of your Unique Strengths.

Keep in mind that the Unique Strengths you see in yourself may be different than the ones others see in you, and may be based on where and how they interacted with you in the past. Throughout your lifetime, you will develop many different and sometimes divergent Unique Strengths, but at the end of the day, there's going to be a super strength you want to lean on and utilize especially when you are challenged with a Transformative Moment or transformative period in your life.

Recognizing a Unique Strength

One night while we were finishing dinner, I asked my daughter, who was in second grade at the time, if her homework was done. She replied with confidence and just a little pride, "Oh sure! It's done."

I said, "I want to see what you're doing." She brought out four pages of paper stapled together. She'd answered all the questions on the first page, and they were all correct. I flipped to the second page, nothing was filled out. Flipped to the third page, nothing was filled out. Flipped to the fourth page, nothing was filled out!

I said, "Samantha, it doesn't look like your homework's complete."

Guilelessly, she replied, "Yeah...I don't need to do the other pages. The teacher never looks beyond the first page." Suppressing a smile, I said, "That's not quite the way it works. You're actually going to do all of your homework." Even though I said this to her, my first instinct was to marvel at what I recognized as her Unique Strength! She'd figured out the game and understood what needed to be done to win it.

As she grew up, I watched that Unique Strength show itself time and again, whether it was setting a goal in school and then figuring out how to achieve it, or dealing calmly with the inherent emotional drama of the teenage years. When approaching a challenge, or a new situation or person, she would lead by asking questions rather than telling anyone what to do. She asked questions to figure out what the situation or "game" was, so that she could find the best and most efficient path to the solution.

Unique Strengths Help You Navigate Transformative Moments

Whenever you experience a challenging moment, particularly a Transformative Moment, you will want to know what your Unique Strength is. Transformative Moments can throw you off your path and prompt you to ask yourself, "What do I really want to do?" In these moments you will want to counter your feelings of insecurity with the question, "What is my Unique Strength, and how can I leverage it so I can be successful doing what makes me happy?"

Often, when you're hit with a Transformative Moment, you're also hit with self-doubt, which can easily derail you and make you feel helpless, or like a victim of circumstance. By focusing on your Unique Strength, you can empower yourself by leveraging your assets. This will protect your confidence, which will enable you to access the energy, clarity and courage to pursue whatever new Vision for your future arises as you navigate the Transformative Moment.

THE FOUR STAGES OF LEARNING

You are constantly experiencing new events and moments throughout your life, and you are constantly learning new things. It's important for you to recognize that you are always in one of the Four Stages of Learning (originally developed by Gordon Training International) regardless of what you are learning or what you know. You may be at different stages in different areas in your life, but you are always in one of the following stages:

1. **Unconscious Incompetence**—You don't know what you don't know.

2. **Conscious Incompetence**—You realize that you don't know what you need to know.
3. **Conscious Competence**—You know what to do, but you need to think first.
4. **Unconscious Competence**—Everything is on reflex.

Your Unique Strength is going to grow and change over the course of time. You may find that you will need to go through a learning process, perhaps even one that is rigorous, in order to optimize your Unique Strength. It can sometimes take years to get to the **Unconscious Competence Stage**. At the very least, it takes practice. As Malcolm Gladwell asserts in his book, *Outliers: The Story of Success*, it can take over 10,000 hours of practice to perfect something. It just makes sense...the more you do something, the better you get at it.

EXERCISE
DISCOVERING YOUR UNIQUE STRENGTH

STEP 1: Write down what you think your "Unique Strength" is...your strength above all other strengths.

STEP 2: Then—this next step might seem scary—ask five (or more) people what they see as your Unique Strength. Pick a variety of people who will be honest with you. I encourage you to let go of any self-judgment and just be open and curious about what you might hear back from them.

STEP 3: When you figure out who your five (or more) people will be, explain what you're looking for by saying (emailing) something like the following:

> Hi _____,
>
> I'm doing a project and could use your help...it should only take a minute or two. If you had to describe my Unique Strength, what would you say it is? It should be that strength above all other strengths you think comes naturally for me.
>
> I appreciate you taking the time to help with this project. I'll explain more about it later.

STEP 4: If you find yourself fearful of this exercise... pause, and ask yourself, "Why am I fearful?" Write down why you feel fearful. Is fear controlling you or preventing you from achieving the life you want to live? We will revisit this in the next few chapters, but in the meantime, feel the fear and do it anyway. Go for it! Ask five people what your Unique Strength is. Just do it!

STEP 5: Make a list of all the responses you receive.

"If you can perceive it and believe it, you can achieve it."

~ Napoleon Hill

CHAPTER THREE

YOUR VISION

Designing Your Future

WHY IT IS IMPORTANT TO HAVE A VISION

I was on the varsity baseball team during my freshman year at Oregon State. At the beginning of practice that fall, the coach addressed our team. With great enthusiasm, he stated, "We have two goals for this season. The first is to win the Pac-10 North Division." (Baseball was divided into North and South Divisions during those years.) "The second is to get to Regionals." Everyone on the team felt fired up by the coach's determination to reach these goals.

Rainy Oregon wasn't considered a baseball state like Arizona and California where teams could practice outside all year round, so these goals seemed realistic to the team. I sat there listening to the coach, but wondered to myself why our goal wasn't getting to and winning the College World Series. That would have been the ultimate goal!

We won the Pac-10 and went to Regionals, but then lost in the semi-finals. On the plane ride home I heard players saying things like, "We were one game away from going to the World Series. We were so close."

After listening to these players, I turned to a fellow pitcher and said, "Wasn't our goal to win the Pac-10 North Division and get to the Regionals? We did that."

He said, "Yeah, but we were so close to the College World Series!"

I replied, "<u>That</u> should have been our goal. We would have gotten there."

We had a great team, we had great coaches, and we had achieved our goals. So, what was the problem?

When I look back on this, I recognize that our perception of what was possible was completely based on our limited beliefs about what was possible. These were beliefs that had been formed by our individual and collective experiences. We were envisioning what we thought was possible, based in part on what we thought was NOT possible. Therein lies the problem. We had unconsciously, but intentionally, limited our success by manifesting an outcome based mainly on what we believed to be attainable.

BELIEFS CAN BE LIMITING OR EMPOWERING

I see this same phenomenon playing out all the time in every area of life. Our limiting (rather than empowering) beliefs often inform and create our Visions, which means they are based on whatever we perceive to be realistic or acceptable. Often, far into adulthood, we base our perceptions, choices, and actions on limiting beliefs we picked up when we were children. We were programmed to believe what we believe, and these beliefs are based on our experiences, as well as on the influences of our parents, teachers, schoolmates, cultural institutions, and of course, the media. Our limiting beliefs can prevent us from staying open to what is <u>actually</u> possible.

Listen carefully to the people around you and note how often they make statements like: "I can't do that." or "That's impossible." This mindset is contagious. Pay attention to how you feel when you hear people using phrases like these. Do you feel inspired by them? Do you feel empowered? My hunch is that you don't.

You will also hear people repeating phrases like: "Yes, let's do it!" or "I think we can." How do you feel around these people? For most, these phrases are energizing and empowering. Remember to pay attention to the words coming out of your mouth. Are they expressing positive and therefore empowering beliefs and thoughts (energy giving), or negative and therefore limiting beliefs and fears (energy taking)?

The first step is committing yourself to being energy giving. The second step is identifying your Unique Strengths, which will give you the confidence to face

Transformative Moments. The third step in supporting yourself is to identify and describe your Vision—where are you headed and why. The baseball team that didn't make it to the College World Series, but came very close, just never saw themselves capable of getting there to begin with.

THE LAW OF ATTRACTION

My family and I were spending Christmas in Hawaii, so I attended a Christmas service at a little church in Lahaina on the island of Maui. It was a beautiful Hawaiian morning, warm with a gentle breeze blowing through the church. The priest was talking about how the coming year was going to be the "year of hope." I found this unsettling because I've always felt that "hoping" was passive and indicative of a victim mentality. In other words, rather than working to create your destiny, you just sit around and "hope" things will go your way.

I feel that a better word or concept is "belief." As in, "It is my belief that I'm creating what I want in my life," or "I believe that I'm achieving the future I'm envisioning." These sentences demonstrate the potential positive impact of the empowering belief, rather than the negative impact of the limiting belief, which we just explored. By consciously taking control of your beliefs, rather than allowing the limiting beliefs you unconsciously picked up from your family and community to guide your choices, you give yourself the opportunity to take control of your destiny. You empower yourself!

When you use the word "hope," you're leaving room for something not to happen. When you say, "I believe..." you're making a commitment to yourself to make whatever you want happen by doing whatever is necessary to head in the direction of your intended outcome. "Believe" is a powerful word. It's a reminder that you must choose your intentions wisely.

I should probably blame the game of baseball for giving me that perspective early on. I remember when I stood on the baseball mound, I always thought, "I <u>believe</u> I'm going to get these hitters out." I never thought, "I <u>hope</u> I get the hitters out today." I had learned at an early age that if I didn't believe it, it wasn't going to happen. And sure, I gave up a hit to a batter from time to time, but I always believed I was going to get the next hitter out and ultimately win the game.

Your thoughts, words and physical actions will follow what your brain focuses on. If you are about to go on stage and give a speech to a group of strangers and you really believe that you are going to "nail it," more often than not, you will. Your behaviors generally follow what you believe. This book is not asking you to change what you believe, it's asking you to take the time to discover WHY you believe what you do. What you believe has a direct impact on your Vision of what is possible and the choices you make in pursuit of your Vision.

When you have an understanding of how beliefs manifest themselves, you will also understand how to stay open to what's really possible, and how to steer your focus toward the positive, empowering beliefs that will support your Vision. With positive beliefs, a strong intention, and a clear Vision, you can achieve most anything, and usually a lot faster than you ever expected.

OFF TO CHASE RABBITS...

While I was president of an online marketing and sales consulting company, I started working with a young woman named Betsy, who was the account manager for one of our partner vendors. For two years she reported metrics and results to us on a monthly basis, then one day out of the blue I got an email from her with a subject line that read: "Off to chase rabbits."

When Betsy started working with our company she was twenty-two, and recently out of college, where she'd been the president of her sorority. She was a classic overachiever who'd gotten straight A's her whole life. She was great at servicing our account and our company, but I could always tell she was trying to figure out whether this was really what she wanted to be doing for the rest of her life.

So, I wasn't completely surprised when I got the "chasing rabbits" email. I sent her back an email asking, "Which rabbits are you off to chase?" She replied that she was going into the health and fitness world to help people transform their bodies in a healthy way. Her intention was to create a custom meal and exercise program for her clients and then monitor their progress through texts and emails in order to help them achieve their goals.

I thought her plan sounded interesting, and I needed to shed a few pounds, so I suggested that I become one of her first clients. She worked with me for a couple of months, and I was getting healthier and fitter, then she disappeared. I assumed that she was probably off trying to figure out what her next step or move was going to be.

After about nine months, I got another email out of the blue that said something like, "I don't know what I want to do." I called Betsy and she told me she was suffering from "Quarter Life Crisis." It was evident to me that she was experiencing the same thing so many other young people I'd interviewed over the years had experienced. I had also witnessed the fallout of this "crisis," which is characterized by anxiety about how life is going to turn out, in my own daughter.

I told Betsy about Project OTY and asked her if she would like to be one of the first students to go all the way through the program. She enthusiastically agreed to go through the curriculum outlined in this book, which is the core of Project OTY. We started by identifying her Unique Strengths. It turned out that Betsy's Unique Strength was her ability to project an energy ball of positivity that drew people to her. In addition to this super power, I identified another one of her Unique Strengths—her ability to learn at a rapid pace. These were the Strengths she was going to be able to leverage to create the kind of life she wanted to live.

In the initial process, we turned the conversation from WHAT she wanted in life, to HOW she wanted to live her life, and HOW we could make that possible. Betsy spent a weekend working on her Vision. She listed twenty bullet points that described her Vision. Her bullet points were distributed among various categories such as, career, health, finances, family, and so on. I told Betsy to dream as big as she wanted! The next step was to establish a timeframe for her Vision. We chose to make it a ten-year Vision for a few reasons. The biggest reason was that it removed the pressure of having to make it happen NOW. It also removed the stress of having a Vision, because there was now plenty of time to work toward achieving it.

Betsy's initial Vision bullet points did not feel entirely authentic to her. Part of why it had been difficult for her to figure out what she wanted to do was that she wasn't totally in touch with her <u>authentic</u> Vision. Her need for approval had made her into a lifelong overachiever. She felt tremendous pressure to be the best, but her definition of "the best" was almost completely unattainable.

When she really began to clarify her Vision, I brought up the possibility that she might be trying to conform to someone else's Vision. I encouraged her to explore whether her Vision was authentic to her, or perhaps influenced by her network of parents, friends and teachers, or even by general societal and cultural expectations. I wanted her to explore why she believed what she believed, and where these beliefs came from.

She did a few exercises (which will be outlined in the next couple of chapters) that encouraged her to look closely at her Vision bullet points and the motivations behind them, which helped her clarify for herself the bullet points that she felt were most authentic to her. She ultimately created a list of Vision bullet points she was genuinely excited about pursuing. This is one of the most important aspects of the entire program: you've got to develop an idea of what you want <u>your</u> world to look like!

EXERCISE
FORMULATING YOUR VISION

In this exercise, you are going to work on the first version of your Vision. You may find yourself questioning your Vision as you work it out. The natural tendency is to come up with reasons or excuses as to why it may not happen. Try not to judge at this point whether your Vision is possible. Spend as much time as you want on this exercise. I encourage you to give this exercise the attention it deserves.

As you go through these steps, KEEP IN MIND, this is YOUR VISION! This is not what others think you should do. You need a Vision that YOU are passionate about. This is an exercise in creating a Vision for the life YOU want to live, not the life that others might want you to live. It's YOUR life, isn't it?

STEP 1: Find a quiet spot to sit and work.

STEP 2: Close your eyes. Think about what you want your life to <u>look like</u> in TEN years. If ten years feels too far way, then focus on five years. The reason for creating a ten-year Vision plan is to remove the stress of time from the equation, and put yourself in a better position to see and recognize how to deal with your current life pressures.

It has been my observation that the only time we feel stress in our lives is when time is controlling us, or when we are trying to control time. By giving ourselves the gift of time, we can be more patient with ourselves and our process, and find more joy in the current moments as we navigate through them toward our Vision.

What do you want your life to look like in five or ten years? Think about everything. It does not matter how big your dreams are. DO NOT EDIT this version of your Vision. Just dream. Dream BIG!

STEP 3: After you have formulated your Vision for your life in your head, write down in bullet point format everything you just dreamed. Everything. Categorize if you'd like: Home, Family, Spouse/Partner, Friends, Job, Money, Health, Activities, Travel, Toys, Gifts to Give, Hobbies…

Write down at least twenty things. And don't worry about how things are going to happen. That is when we run into trouble. Just describe what you want your life to look like. Remember to write in bullet points. And remember that your Vision is not about what you want, but about how you want to live. You cannot "want" something into your life, but you can create a Vision and make the choices that lead you in the direction of your dreams and desires.

After you list your twenty Vision bullet points, you may realize that you have no idea how your Unique Strengths are going to help you accomplish them. **There is not always an obvious correlation between your Unique Strengths and your Vision.** Although I encourage you to take your Unique Strengths into consideration when developing your Vision, in order to fully realize your Vision, you will likely need to seek out the assistance of others. (We will discuss this at length in a later chapter.)

Your Vision should be:
- Something you can remember and envision.
- A dream you can share with others.
- Inspirational!

"Feel the fear and do it anyway."

~ Susan Jeffers

CHAPTER FOUR

EGO, FEARS AND MOTIVATIONS

Why Do You Do Those Things You Do?

FACING FEAR

I was with ten Canadians and four Americans in the middle of nowhere—also known as Pecos, New Mexico. Our company (headquartered out of Vancouver, BC) had flown our top performers to a retreat center in Pecos for an event called "Winners Circle." Six months earlier the company had sent us on a three-day cruise to Mexico, and six months before that, on a three-day blitz in Las Vegas. In this remote high desert town, there was literally nowhere for a bunch of twenty-somethings to party. We were stuck actually having to communicate with each other, which turned out to be a good thing, since we would be engaging in a variety of trust exercises over the weekend.

The morning after we arrived, I walked down to the ropes course. Being an athlete, I assumed it would be fun and easy. The first event required each person to stand on a six-foot platform and fall backwards into their team members' arms. It wasn't a big drop and everyone on our team, except for one woman, did it. This woman, who probably weighed only about 100 pounds, was terrified at the idea of falling backwards into our arms. She just couldn't do it. My first instinct was to privately judge her. Then I became curious as to <u>why</u> this seemingly easy exercise was so terrifying for her. I wanted to find out and understand what was underlying or motivating her fear.

The next event was the telephone pole. I strapped myself into the safety gear and climbed up the pole. I'm 6' 2" and weighed about 225 pounds at the time, but I had no problem climbing up to the top. When I got there, I had to step up onto the top of the telephone pole, which was only 14" in diameter. In that moment, I unexpectedly found myself in the biggest battle with my mind I had ever experienced in my life. It was like in the movies when you see a devil sitting on one shoulder, and an angel on the other.

I can do this... I'm an athlete. Yeah...but I'm also 50 feet up in the air. What about the safety gear...if I fall it will catch me. Does the safety gear know I'm 225 pounds? When was it last tested? Is it still even on me? I can't feel it. There's slack in the line. I just saw Fred do this, and he was just fine... I'll be fine too. There's no f-ing way. This is crazy! The boss is down there...I need to show him I'm not afraid.

Wow... I was having such an intense internal battle! But throughout this, I just kept slowly moving up the pole and eventually somehow I ended up standing on top of the pole. I'm sure you could hear my knees banging together all the way to the East Coast. I was scared to death.

The instructor at the bottom yelled up, "Okay... pause for a moment and listen to your inner voice."

In my head, I was thinking... *I've been listening to that f-ing voice scream at me for the last five minutes, you idiot.* That voice was still running through a thousand different scenarios, none of them good...*Fall and die. Fall and strangle myself. Fall and break a leg. Fall and crush my ribs...Or... finally...jump and be lowered down safely.*

I went for it! I jumped! And it was no biggie! I made it down in one piece.

Over the next ten years, I spent a considerable amount of time studying psychology, human behavior, sales, marketing, and neuroscience. When I learned that our decisions are essentially driven by the oldest part of our brains, I really started to connect all the dots. At the back of the brain, we have a need to feel "safe." It's a survival instinct. The tricky part about this is that what we define as safe or not, is completely based on our beliefs. Our beliefs originate from all of our unique experiences, moments and influences, and since no two people have experienced all the same things, we each have a very particular idea of what is safe and what is not.

It turned out that the woman who couldn't allow herself to fall backwards into the arms of her teammates had fallen out of a tree when she was a young girl and broken her back. What do you learn when you get curious about other people's stories? You learn very quickly that everyone is dealing with something. Each of us is influenced by, or motivated by, some kind of fear, and each of our fears is based on our fundamental and underlying need to feel safe.

Fear and the Formation of the Ego

Sigmund Freud identified four basic fears that influence all our motivations and form the foundation of our egos or identities:

1. Fear of Loss
2. Fear of Rejection
3. Fear of Failure
4. Fear of Success

These fears are based on our most basic survival instincts as well as our experiences and influences. It's our fears that drive our actions and behaviors, and shape our motivations and decisions. Think about all your experiences in life so far and how they might have generated fear. How did your parents treat you? Did you suffer a loss? Were you criticized? What were your friends like? Did you have friends? What were/are your relationships like with your parents, siblings, teachers, coaches, kids, spouses, friends, bosses?

These influences and experiences all affect how we see ourselves and what we believe about ourselves. What we believe about ourselves can compel us to behave in certain ways, in certain situations, in order to be whatever we have been led to think is acceptable. We develop fears that ultimately drive our behaviors. This often leads us away from being ourselves. Instead we develop an ego projection of who we think we need to be, in order to be liked, loved, approved of, and appreciated. This is one of the ways we stay safe in the world.

Why are we led to believe that one way of being is better than another? Think about all the messaging we have been fed since the day we were born. In the United States, companies spend billions of dollars each year on marketing. This unrelenting messaging reaches us through the media, and it shapes what we believe and value. As a result, what we end up defining as important or valuable is sometimes in alignment with our authentic desires, interests, and drives, and sometimes not. Most of this messaging is speaking to fears and perceived fears, and in many cases it is trying to create a fear. I have found that "fear-based" decision making will NEVER lead you to accomplishing your Vision.

In order to identify whether your Vision is authentically yours (and not your mother's, best friend's, or based on something you've heard or seen on TV or the internet), you need to understand the motivations and fears underlying your desires, and how all of these aspects work together to form and support your ego. Your ego can protect your vulnerabilities and give you a presence in the world. It can be a true representation of your most confident, genuine self, the part of you that faces your challenges with faith and the willingness to do what it takes to move forward with your life. However, your ego can also be a mask, the persona you hide behind, a misrepresentation of your true self. It can be the posture you adopt to compensate for feeling unworthy or unlovable.

We all have an ego, and it is not intrinsically negative or positive. The ego is created by a complex combination of factors—environmental, social, hereditary—that continue to influence you throughout your life. The reality is that your ego is a reflection of why you are the type of person you are. If your influences have been positive, and you have felt supported and encouraged in your life, you may very well be more inclined to develop an open, accepting disposition, and a high sense of self-regard. Your ego, your presentation of your personality, may come across as sincere and confident. You may have more inner resources for dealing with adversity. You may be good at managing your fears.

On the other hand, if you have not felt supported in your life and/or come from an environment in which you have felt diminished or put down, you may very well develop an ego that either compensates for your perceived lacks, or an ego that projects your sense of inferiority. In other words, you may come across as a know-it-all with a bombastic delivery, or an insecure wall-flower with a self-deprecating manner.

Your ego can either serve your highest interests and propel you onward, or keep you spinning in your own circle of self-denial and even self-hatred, or both...Most of us have had both experiences. We have felt confident in our integrity as we have moved forward toward a goal that is in alignment with our inner truth, and we have blustered, faked and bullied our way into situations we thought would serve us. The question is, how can we get the ego to serve our authentic interests? How can we get our actions and behaviors, our motivations and impulses, to be in alignment with our most genuine, heart-felt desires? How can we best support our truest goals?

How I Became a Baseball Player

I was sitting in our cozy, wood paneled family room, fire simmering in the brick fireplace, playing *Pong* on the TV. (This was in the '70s, before *Donkey Kong* and *Ms. Pac-Man*, and of course long before *World of Warcraft*.) My dad came in and we flipped the channel to watch the Chicago Cubs play the Cincinnati Reds. Cincinnati was a powerhouse at the time.

My dad mentioned that enrollment for little league was happening the following week and asked if I wanted to sign up.

I said, "No way!"

He was a bit surprised, probably because we were always playing catch in the backyard, so he asked me why.

I said rather emphatically, "I can't play baseball in front of all those people!"

He asked with some confusion, "All what people?"

I pointed to the TV and all the people sitting in the stands. I don't remember him laughing, but I'm pretty sure he was cracking up inside.

He said, "Oh Jeff... the only people who will be at your little league games will be parents of the players and maybe a few friends or grandparents. You're not going to have 60,000 people at your game."

I thought about this for a moment and said, "Okay then... I'll play."

I was only nine, but I was already fearful of how I would need to perform to satisfy all the fans. I saw them booing on TV and it didn't seem like it was making the players on the field feel very good. That was what I wanted to avoid when I first said I didn't want to play little league. I had a fear of rejection.

Managing Fears

This chapter is not about whether or not you have fears. Everybody has them. It's about how you can recognize and understand them, so that you can overcome them or effectively manage them in order to create your Vision.

In the last chapter we talked about the people who are energy takers, the ones who say things like, "I can't do that." or "That won't work." or "That's impossible." Well, it's the same thing when we're talking to ourselves, when we're telling ourselves, "I can't do that. That would be impossible for me. There is no way I can do that." When we say these things to ourselves, we are sapping our strength, taking our own energy away from our Vision. That's really what we need to manage.

I'm not a psychologist, but I do believe that you must first understand your fears before you can manage them. Based on my experiences, I have found that the entire process laid out in this book is a roadmap to <u>managing</u> your fears, and <u>understanding</u> your fears begins with going through the following step-by-step process:

1. Acknowledge and honor the fact that you have fears. Then allow yourself to FEEL your fear.
2. In order to identify which fear you're feeling, ask yourself:

- Am I feeling a...Fear of Failure?
- Am I feeling a...Fear of Rejection?
- Am I feeling a...Fear of Loss?
- Am I feeling a...Fear of Success?

3. Ask yourself honestly how and why your fears came about. Be aware of the stories you tell yourself to make yourself feel good. As humans we develop stories to compensate for our fears, and they are ultimately reflected in the ego we portray. Managing your fears is about being honest with yourself, so that you will have better insight into what may steer you away from your Vision, as well as what will ultimately lead you in the direction of your Vision. Call it an exercise in honestly looking at yourself in the mirror. If you can't be honest with yourself, who can you be honest with?

4. Ask yourself questions in order to really understand how or why you might feel a certain fear in some situations but not in others. The question to keep asking is: "Why am I defining this (whatever this is) to be safe or not." It will push you to consider all the influences that have shaped who you are. It's imperative to take the time to explore why you do what you

do, and why you say what you say. It is only then that you will be equipped to manage your fears going forward in a manner that supports your progress in the direction of your Vision.

WHO'S PILOTING YOUR CRAFT?

I was flying back to Portland from Salt Lake City, on my way home from a seminar I'd conducted for some of our new sales staff. I was teaching them sales techniques and had emphasized how important it is to "feel the fear" and pick up the phone anyway. In that training seminar someone had mentioned that **FEAR** could be read as an acronym for: **False Events Appear Real**.

On the flight I happened to be sitting next to a youngish businessman. We started talking and he told me he was also from Portland and was headed home. Like a lot of people, he was a nervous flyer. Every bump, every turn of the plane, every minor dip or engine noise caused him to tense up and grip the armrest. I asked him if he flew a lot. He said he flew every few months for work but didn't like it. He said he had a "fear of flying."

I asked him, "Do you have a fear of flying, or do you have a fear of crashing and dying?"

I could tell he was irritated by my question at first, but then he paused and thought about it for a moment. He said, "I suppose I like the idea of flying... but I don't like the idea of crashing and dying."

We continued talking, and I learned that he had a wife and a young child. We talked about raising kids and the stresses that go along with the responsibility to provide for them. He wanted to make sure his child attended private school, got into a good college, got a good job and so forth. It turned out that his child was only two years old, but he had already mapped out her entire life.

When I asked him what it was about crashing and dying that he was afraid of, he said it was the thought that he would never get to see his child grow up, and never get to see his wife, family, and friends again. He would lose them forever. I asked him if he thought his flying anxieties might be motivated by the "Fear of Loss."

He said, "Definitely. That's it."

I reminded him that we always bump a little bit approaching Portland as the plane drops below the Columbia Gorge winds. He actually relaxed a little bit. We landed safely and when we got up to grab our bags from the overhead compartment, he said, "Thank you. It wasn't until now that I realized how fearful I was of dying and losing my family. It wasn't until this flight that I realized how much the death of my own father at a young age impacted how I think and feel."

I said, "No problem... just remember... 'False Events Appear Real' when FEAR is controlling us."

Wait... What about Love?

I was explaining the impact that fear plays in our lives and our decision making process to a friend. My friend felt strongly that her motivations throughout her life have not been based on fear as much as they have been based on love. I told her that I too feel motivated by love and want to help others as often as I can, but I also see how fear underlies my impulse to express love. The way fear motivates us to act, and its relationship to the need to feel safe is often highly complex and can show up in subtle ways.

At an early age, we learn what makes us feel safe and what doesn't. Our influences and experiences are powerful in determining who we become and what we believe. When we share love, we often receive love, acceptance, and some form of positive feedback. When we receive love and/or positive feedback, it generally makes us feel good. When we feel good, we feel safe, which satisfies one of our basic core instincts.

So, is it love that motivates us, or is it the fear that we may not feel love in return if we don't give love, that motivates us? Freud would have classified this as <u>fear of rejection</u>, because receiving love in return for love given is a sign of acceptance. Not all fears are "run for the hills" type fears. In some cases, they are very subtle and we may even experience difficulty recognizing them at a conscious level. Discovering and identifying the fear behind your motivations can often require you to think deeply, and explore why you do what you do and believe what you believe.

Another friend asked about her motivation to see a particular concert that was coming to town.

She asked, "How is fear motivating me to see this concert?"

Fear is subtle and the answer is not always obvious, but our fears are designed to protect us so we feel safe.

I asked her, "Why is seeing this concert important to you?"

She replied, "It will be entertaining."

I asked her why being entertained was important to her. Her reply was that this particular band's music made her feel good. I asked her why feeling good mattered. She said that it made her happy. I asked her what she felt when she was happy. She said being happy made her feel...safe! So you see, if she missed this concert for some reason, she was going to miss an opportunity to be entertained, feel happy, and feel safe. This motivation was being driven by the <u>fear of loss</u>.

Professional sales people and marketers know how powerful this feeling of loss can be. In fact, a sales closing technique designed to prey on this fear is used quite frequently in the sales game. It is called the "Standing Room Only" close. The concept is, that if you don't act now, you are going to lose your opportunity to have, buy, and acquire whatever is being sold.

EXERCISE
EGO, FEARS AND MOTIVATIONS

All motivations, at their core, are being driven by one of the four fears. So, whatever you want to pursue, ultimately boils down to managing one of these fears.

It starts with <u>why</u>. I've always believed that it does not matter <u>what</u> happens in life, or what people do. What matters is, why. Why did you write down the twenty bullet points in the Vision that you listed? <u>Why</u>? When we understand why things come to be, and pay attention to why things are the way they are, we find that we are able to connect more with everything and everybody. We find that solutions to difficult problems can be solved and exceptional opportunities can be pursued in the direction of our Vision. We are better able to recognize, manage and break through any real or perceived fears in our way.

Not every fear is necessarily negative. It's okay to embrace some fear. It's okay to recognize that a lot of the decisions you're making are based on these fears, but what's more important is that you connect with how your fears developed. The motivation to find shelter stems from a fundamental fear that you can probably figure out for yourself. On the other hand, why might you be motivated to live in a mansion by the lake with a boat and Ferrari? What's the fear that's driving your desire?

Ask yourself a lot of <u>why</u> questions...dig into your subconscious to really understand why one bullet point might be more important to you than the others. What's the real motivation? The real fear? By getting in touch with the fears that are actually pushing you to chase these motivations, you can then take a step back and start to connect them to why and how your fears came to be in the first place.

You'll start to see that your fears are based not only on events and moments, but how you've been taught to interpret them as well. You'll be able to begin to understand this and start to become more authentic with yourself. You may even find that your Vision changes a little bit.

STEP 1: Look at each bullet point in your Vision.

    a. Write down the <u>MOTIVATION</u> for each Vision bullet point.
    b. Under the Motivation, write down the <u>FEAR</u> that drives this Motivation. (Fear of... Failure, Loss, Rejection, or Success.)
    c. Under the Fear, write down <u>WHY</u> this fear exists and <u>HOW</u> it came to be.

EXAMPLE:

VISION BULLET POINT: To work at a job I love.

MOTIVATION: I'll be happy because I'll have a sense of purpose in life.

FEAR TO MANAGE: Fear of Failure

WHY: If I don't find a job I love, I'll be wasting my potential just struggling to get through my day. I'll feel like a failure because I won't be doing anything I feel is meaningful. I've always wanted to make a difference and see the impact of my work.

STEP 2: Go through each Vision bullet point and evaluate what you wrote under Motivation, Fear and Why. Now, prioritize each bullet point in your Vision according to the level of importance it has for you. Number one is most important to you. Number twenty is least important.

"If one advances confidently in the direction of his dreams,

and endeavors to live the life which he has imagined,
he will meet with success unexpected in common hours."
~ Henry David Thoreau

CHAPTER FIVE

CRYSTALIZING YOUR VISION

Painting the Picture of What You Truly Want

When I was in the employment industry, my goal was to make a successful placement with the client. In order to do this, I needed to fully understand the skills and abilities of the potential employee along with his or her goals, overall background and current situation. I also needed to understand what the client was looking for. To make these matches work, I asked a lot of questions of the job applicants until I understood **what** they were looking for, **how** they saw their needs being met by a certain position, and most importantly, **why** they wanted a particular job. I found that the people who genuinely understood their Unique Strengths and could best articulate their Vision were the folks who went on to have the most success.

Your Vision defines and describes the life you want to create for yourself, and you cannot achieve your Vision without the help of other people. If your Vision is crystal clear, you will be in a stronger position to paint a picture of it in order to attract the support and assistance of others. In this chapter, you will learn how to precisely and vividly imagine and articulate an inspiring portrait of your Vision. You want to not only clarify for yourself that your Vision is indeed YOUR Vision, you want to be able to inspire others to help you move toward it and ultimately achieve it. In Chapter Six you will learn about how to use this crystalized Vision to "enroll" the assistance of those whose Unique Strengths complement your own, thereby creating a "win-win" opportunity.

Crystalizing your Vision will help you feel strong and confident when you are communicating your Vision to others. Clarity erases fear, doubt and uncertainty, and helps other people learn about you more quickly. A crystal clear Vision not only empowers you, but it empowers others who may stand to benefit from the Vision you are sharing with them. We all crave transparency because it helps us understand what we are dealing with in the moment, which allows us to make more informed decisions, and then enables us to move forward with confidence because we feel safe doing so.

Is Your Vision Really Your Vision?

During a leadership and personal development workshop I was attending, I heard someone say, "We generally make a lot of decisions to either 'look good' or avoid 'looking bad.'"

That comment made sense to me. It falls into alignment with the idea that we are primarily motivated by the four fears (loss, rejection, failure and success) discussed in the previous chapter. Not only that, but whatever we define as "looking good" or "looking bad" is completely based on the unique moments, influences, and experiences we have had over the course of a lifetime. For each one of us, the definition of "looking good" or "looking bad" is going to be different.

When you think about your Vision, and the motivations and fears that drive you, and WHY they drive you, you start to understand how your Vision came to be. Many people are chasing a Vision not because they are passionate about it, but because they believe it's the right thing to do, or they have been led to believe that it's a Vision worth pursuing. I've seen many people chasing Visions that are not necessarily their own. It's still not unusual to find young people pursuing the same careers their parents have chosen. I'm not saying this is a bad thing, but are their choices authentic? When you look forward to the future, you need to consider whether you are chasing a Vision that you are passionate about, or a Vision someone else is passionate about.

This next step is critical. We are going to crystallize your Vision. Think about the messages you've been fed since you were young. Think about what you have been led to believe. The point of this exercise is not to judge whether what you've been told is right or wrong, but to recognize whether the Vision you are chasing is really yours.

It's your life, right? So it seems to me that it's important for you to:

1. Know whether YOUR Vision is YOUR Vision...or not.
2. Understand why your Vision is important to you.
3. Know what fears you are going to need to manage in order to achieve your Vision.
4. Be able to describe your Vision so people can see it with you.
5. Create a Vision that you truly believe in.

When you were asked to write down your Vision bullet points, it was suggested that these be bullet points you really believe in and believe you can achieve. If you don't believe you can achieve your Vision bullet points, they are just wishes and hopes.

I was explaining this concept to a friend and he said, "You can't predict the future just because you believe it will happen." I explained that this is not an exercise in predicting the future. It is an exercise in pursuing a Vision that YOU are passionate about pursuing. It's about identifying the best life you believe is achievable, and then taking the steps to create it.

Your crystallized Vision will keep you focused and moving forward with intention. This doesn't mean that everything will always work out exactly the way you imagine it will, but you will find that when you are moving forward with intention, you will be able to create and attract more of what you are looking for in your life.

THE POWER OF INTENTION TO CREATE NEW OPPORTUNITIES

The clearer your Vision, the more focused your intention. The power of living with intention is that your actions and decisions become purpose-driven. By crystalizing your Vision, you set the stage to move forward, and you'll find that new, and often unexpected opportunities will come into your life. What you make them mean will evolve as you consider how these new possibilities might tie into your Vision.

As these new opportunities manifest in many unique ways and often very quickly, you have to practice staying open to learning from them. If you are passionate about your Vision, you can very quickly identify whether a new situation, person or seeming opportunity is going to push you toward your Vision or away from it. Don't worry about exactly how your Vision will manifest itself. When you look back years later, you will see the dots that connected your journey. You will see the Transformative Moments that have impacted your life. This book is about anticipating and managing your Transformative Moments going forward. It's a process that will help you regain focus and allow you the opportunity to pursue your Vision with purposeful intention. It's a process that will allow you to create YOUR world.

As you go through this process of Crystallizing your Vision, you may start to wonder why certain things have not happened already, or why something else has happened instead. Do NOT let this self-questioning derail you. When you understand that pursuing a Vision is a journey, you will find that you become more accepting of that journey, and in the process it becomes easier to learn from the past in order to create the future you want.

This is YOUR Vision. It does not need to be perfect. It will morph and evolve along with you. By crystallizing your Vision and really having a passion for what you've chosen, you put yourself in the position to be your best self because you're clear about what you value. You're creating a roadmap you have defined as being important to you, which will direct all the choices you'll make moving forward.

EXERCISE
CRYSTALIZING YOUR VISION

This book and these exercises are about recognizing where you are currently, where you want to go and how to get there. Spend some time on this exercise. Do NOT rush it, and if you are rushing it, ask yourself... why? Take time to think about your Vision <u>clearly</u> and <u>specifically</u>. The goal is to develop some conviction around this Vision. When you get fully committed to the practice of visioning, you'll find that it generally won't take ten years to achieve most of what you have identified in your Vision bullet points.

You are going to rewrite your Vision. It's time to crystallize it. You're going to get specific with this. Crystal clear.

STEP 1: Look at each bullet point in your Vision list. Ask yourself again, "Why is this important to me?" Is it because YOU really believe it is important? Is it because others believe it is important? Ask these sorts of questions of yourself:

- What is my real motivation?
- Why do I want to do this?
- How did this develop?
- Why did this become important to me?

- Why is being a _____ important to me?
- Why is having a _____ important to me?

Keep digging so that you really start to get to the true motivation behind your Vision. When you start to dig, you will find that aspects of your Vision are often based on some influence outside of yourself, or based on something that somebody else has convinced you to believe is important.

STEP 2: Remove any Vision bullet points that you are not 100% committed to. Remove those that you do not believe are really important to YOU, or those that you cannot picture. The picture should be crystal clear in your mind.

STEP 3: If you have any "I want" items on your list, change them to "I will" items, or remove them if you are not truly committed.

STEP 4: Feel free to add more bullet points if you see anything else in your Vision. Keep in mind that you can change your Vision over time, as often as you need to transform. The objective is to have your crystal clear Vision in mind at all times.

STEP 5: Rewrite the list and come to a final set of Vision bullet points to which YOU are committed. Under these bullet points write the updated Motivation, and Fear you will have to manage if they have changed during the crystallization process.

STEP 6: NOW...write several short sentences for each bullet point. Paint the picture in words. Remember that you are going to want to clearly, authentically, and enthusiastically articulate your Vision to others.

EXAMPLE:

VISION BULLET POINT: To work at a job I love.

MOTIVATION: I'll be happy because I'll have a sense of purpose in life.

FEAR TO MANAGE: Fear of Failure

WHY: If I don't find a job I love, I'll be wasting my potential just struggling to get through my day. I'll feel like a failure because I won't be doing anything I feel is meaningful. I've always wanted to make a difference and see the impact of my work.

CRYSTAL CLEAR VISION: I will work at a job where I can use my Unique Strengths, and where I am recognized and appreciated for my talents, energy, and creativity. My work space will be open, organized, creative, and inspiring. I will work with people I like, whose Unique Strengths complement my own. I will never be bored because I will be constantly learning. I will advance in the job quickly and eventually become a leader in my field. I will feel more energized and more satisfied at the end of each day. I will wake up every morning looking forward to my life!

"There's always going to be someone smarter, prettier or more talented. Try to appreciate that."
~ Doug Greenhut

CHAPTER SIX

ENROLLING OTHERS

Getting the Help You Need

I was sitting in Mazatlán—unfortunately not the city in Mexico, but a restaurant in Portland. It was around the corner from my office and served a pretty good tostada salad. I was working on a document and eating some lunch while eavesdropping on four female co-workers from some other company sitting a few tables away. It seemed that three seasoned co-workers were treating the newest employee to lunch.

They were talking about where they grew up, how they came to Portland, what their significant others did for work, and so on. What interested me in particular about this conversation was how Vision bullet points and Goals (more on setting and accomplishing Goals in the next chapter) were being discussed. The new employee said she was trying to learn to play golf so she could play with her boyfriend. Her Vision involved spending more time with her boyfriend participating in activities they both enjoyed. Her first Goal toward realizing this

Vision was to learn to play golf, which was something he loved to do.

I heard her say, "I went to the driving range to hit some balls…I guess I was trying to master golf in a day…my hands were bleeding by the time I finished." The others laughed, and she went on, "I know I need to go through the process of learning, but I don't know if I have the time."

One of her lunch mates said, "My husband is a golf pro. If you're really interested, I know he'd love to help. He loves introducing people to the game of golf."

By sharing her Vision and one of her immediate Goals, the wannabe golfer made a connection with someone who offered a possible solution that would significantly reduce the time it would take her to accomplish her Goal. **That is the power of enrolling others in your Vision.** You might be thinking that this sort of thing happens all the time…. and it does. But we usually consider it a fortunate coincidence, and we often call it luck. Imagine if you were able to create these opportunities intentionally. Imagine what you could attract into your life. Imagine what you could accomplish!

Don't get me wrong, this isn't an exercise in manipulating others. This is about discernment, respect, clarity, and transparency. Any type of exchange in which you enlist another's assistance should be a win-win. In other words, both parties should ultimately benefit from the exchange.

I kept listening...The woman who was about to get free golf lessons was thrilled, but a bit reserved about accepting the offer. Her lunch mate insisted, and the new golfer-to-be said, "I can't thank you enough! This will be awesome! I'll pay you back somehow." This told me that she "got it." A "win-win" exchange is about giving as much as you get. Manipulation is about calculatedly leading someone in a direction that only serves your interest. Enrolling someone in your Vision involves openly stating your desires with the intention of enlisting the advice or participation of another person in exchange for whatever they need help accomplishing.

The new golfer-to-be asked what the others were doing for the upcoming Memorial Day weekend. The woman with the golf pro husband said, "I've got eight people coming for the weekend, and I have two big dogs who are shedding everywhere...so I'm looking for a good dog kennel for them." Guess who offered to watch the dogs for the weekend? Yep! The new golfer. It was a win-win, and it happened in the course of normal conversation.

When you can communicate clearly what your Vision bullet points are to others, you will find that you will achieve your Vision much faster than you ever imagined possible. By enrolling others in your Vision, you attract opportunities that you might have never had.

Making the Connection

I was sitting in a gym with about two hundred eighth graders. I asked them to write down on a note card what they wanted their lives to look like when they were eighteen. They each wrote down their Vision. I asked for volunteers to share some of their Vision bullet points. About half of the kids raised their hands and I called on a few.

Grant said, "I want to go to college and study to be a shoe designer so I can work at Nike."

I asked the students, "Does anyone in here know anyone who works at Nike, or knows anything about design?"

A girl raised her hand and said, "My mom works at Nike." I asked her if she thought her Mom would be willing to give Grant any information that might help him become a shoe designer. She said, "I'm sure she would."

Then it was Jennifer's turn. Jennifer wanted to play violin in a rock band. She was evidently pretty good. I asked the kids if anyone knew someone who played music for a living. Derek raised his hand and said that his dad was in a band during college. I asked Derek if he thought his dad could write down a few things for Jennifer to consider when starting a band. Derek said that he thought his dad would help.

Several more students shared their Visions, and in every instance we found someone for them to connect with in order to help them move toward their Vision.

I explained the point of the exercise and how enrolling others would help them achieve their Visions more quickly. The day ended with the students continuing to constructively communicate and share their Visions with one another. It was a powerful and positive scene!

THE PLATINUM RULE

You've probably heard the Golden Rule: "Do to others what you would want them to do to you." However, you may not have heard the Platinum Rule: "Do to others as THEY want done to THEM." Connecting with people and enrolling them is not about you, it's about them. It's about approaching people the way they want to be approached. It's about treating people the way they want to be treated.

No two people are the same. We have all had different moments, events and influences throughout our lives. So it only makes sense that when you are looking to connect with others and enroll them in your Vision, the best way to do this is by understanding what they believe and what they think. By communicating with them the way they need to be communicated with, we then have the opportunity to lead them the way they want to be led.

We don't know what other people want until we ask them questions, listen to their answers and pay attention to their behaviors within the context of our interaction with them. What people do is important. Why they are doing it is even more important. When you understand the Why, you will be in a better position to connect with them the way they want to be connected with. You will find that most people want the same core things in terms of how they want to live, in spite of how different their Visions may be from your own.

How Can I Help You?

When I started working in the employment industry on a regular basis, I had an "aha" moment. I discovered the power of the five word question: How Can I Help You? I realized that most people want to help or need help themselves, but don't know how to offer it or ask for it. Call it Fear of Rejection, or a Fear of Loss. Enrolling others necessitates removing fear from the equation which can be accomplished by leading with questions. When you ask questions, you can better determine how you might be able to help, if help is required, or whether the other person might be available to help you.

Building Your Own Team

In professional sports, the General Manager is often the one who identifies, drafts, and trades players to fill unique rolls within the team. The strongest teams have a number of people with Unique Strengths that complement each other. The players on these teams understand how their Unique Strengths are best utilized, and when they are united with a common Vision, they often do amazing things. We see this all the time in sports teams at all different levels, as well as in teams in other areas of life (business, school, etc.).

We need to build our own team. We need to surround ourselves with people who have Unique Strengths that complement our own if we are to truly achieve our Vision. When you look back at the Vision bullet points you wrote out, it's probably unreasonable to think that you can achieve every one of these on your own. And, even if you can, you will probably need to learn something from someone else.

EXERCISE
ENROLLING OTHERS

Enrolling others is important especially when you are going through a Transformative Moment. People who have Unique Strengths that complement your own will help you achieve your Vision faster than you ever imagined. If you have twenty bullet points, the odds are very good that you will find that at least one, if not several of your bullet points, will connect with just about every person you encounter.

Keep in mind that you will be explaining your Vision to the people you wish to enroll. These people need to be able to help you connect the dots going forward. Not every person you connect with will be able to help you, but some may have valuable insights for you and/or be able to connect you with another person who can help you get to the next step. One person leads to the next.

This may feel uncomfortable at first. So managing your fears is imperative. Have fun!

STEP 1: Review each of your Vision bullet points.

STEP 2: Write down the names of two or more people you feel might be able to help you achieve each bullet point. More than one person might be able to help you with the same bullet point.

EXAMPLE:

VISION BULLET POINT: To work at a job I love.

MOTIVATION: I'll be happy because I'll have a sense of purpose in life.

FEAR TO MANAGE: Fear of Failure

WHY: If I don't find a job I love, I'll be wasting my potential just struggling to get through my day. I'll feel like a failure because I won't be doing anything I feel is meaningful. I've always wanted to make a difference and see the impact of my work.

CRYSTAL CLEAR VISION: I will work at a job where I can use my Unique Strengths, and where I am recognized and appreciated for my talents, energy and creativity. My work space will be open, organized, creative and inspiring. I will work with people I like, and whose Unique Strengths complement my own. I will never be bored, because I will be constantly learning. I will advance in the job quickly and eventually become a leader in my field. I will feel more energized and more satisfied at the end of each day.

I will wake up every morning looking forward to my life!

ENROLL WHO: My friend Steve, a recruiter. Ask him what types of jobs hire people whose Unique Strengths are similar to mine.

"If you want to live a happy life, tie it to a goal."

~ Albert Einstein

Chapter Seven

GOALS

Moving Forward with Your Vision

S.M.A.R.T. Goals

My business associates and I had all been flown into our corporate headquarters for a weekend training workshop. Around me were about twenty young managers and up-and-coming leaders from our offices in Canada and the United States. As much as we all hated giving up a weekend at home, we always got something meaningful out of these trainings.

Our President started our goal planning session by asking us to define what a goal is. People said things like:

> "It's something you want to achieve."
> "It's something you strive for."
> "It's something you measure yourself by."

All the answers were right to some degree, but then she told us that goals need to be "S.M.A.R.T." (George T. Doran) which is an acronym for:

Specific
Measurable
Action-oriented
Reasonable
Timely

As I went through the S.M.A.R.T. exercise and <u>really</u> got specific about the Goals I wanted to achieve, it struck me that there is a difference between a Vision and a Goal. The actual dictionary definitions are:

Vision: A vivid or imaginative conception or anticipation.

Goal: An observable and measurable end result having one or more objectives to be achieved within a more or less fixed timeframe.

It starts with a Vision—a big picture for yourself that defines how you want to live. A Goal is a major milestone in the pursuit of that Vision. A Vision is <u>how</u> you want to live. A Goal tells you if you are on the right path toward that Vision.

To realize your Vision, you need S.M.A.R.T. Goals. Well-defined Goals will have an impact on your choices and behaviors day-to-day. By measuring your progress toward your Vision in terms of Goals, you will be able to recognize which behaviors you may need to alter or modify in pursuit of your Goals and ultimately, your Vision.

A LAZY AFTERNOON AT MCMENAMINS
One evening, I asked my daughter, Sammy, and her high school boyfriend at the time, "What do you want your lives to look like in ten years when you're twenty-six?" They both started to speak with a bit of uncertainty and a lack of clarity about their dreams. They had the typical answers you might expect to hear: "College...good job... make money... have fun...own this or that..." I asked them how they were going to accomplish all this. They both said that they needed to stay in school and get good grades, but neither of them could really articulate the path that would lead to their desired outcomes.

The following Saturday, Sammy, her boyfriend, and I found ourselves sitting in McMenamins out in Rockcreek, a quaint Oregon town tucked in a little valley surrounded by old growth trees. The restaurant is in a refurbished old building with a large stone fireplace. A cozy rustic place. Very Oregon.

During our lunch, I gave Sammy and her boyfriend each a notebook and asked them to write down twenty things that represented how they wanted their lives to look in ten years. They spent about thirty minutes working on this and wrote down all sorts of things, including where they wanted to go to school, where they wanted to live, the type of house they wanted to live in, the kinds of work they wanted to be doing, and the people they wanted in their lives.

For each of their Vision bullet points, I asked them to write out a Goal. I explained the S.M.A.R.T. approach, and told them that each of their Goals had to be **Specific, Measurable, Action-oriented, Reasonable and Timely.** I noticed that they were having a hard time figuring out how long it should take to achieve their Goals. This created a lack of clarity in their ability to fully articulate these Goals and see how they were going to achieve their Visions.

I had forgotten to share with them that each of their Goals should be one-year Goals. Giving themselves twelve months in which to achieve each one of their Goals removed the obstacle of determining what the most important Goal was at the time of the exercise. I told them that they also needed to be clear about what achieving their Goal would look like in twelve months from now. When I clarified this point, it removed the stress of time, and the anxiety associated with it. After they redefined their Goals, we discussed whether or not each Goal was in alignment with the Vision bullet points they had written down.

Goals

As we drove home through the farmlands of Oregon back toward Portland, I asked them if they'd enjoyed the exercises. They both immediately said, "Yes!" I asked them why, and they said it was the first time they felt like they were working on themselves, their future selves. They explained that it wasn't the same old boring stuff they were learning in school.

Many young adults are finding it difficult to see how what they are doing in the moment will have an impact on their futures. Our world has transformed. Our younger generations are asking more questions. They want to understand how what they are doing is tied to the Big Picture. They want to understand why what they are doing in school or their work is important. They want to understand the purpose. We all do. We all want to remove the noise in our lives that doesn't matter. Creating clear Goals helps us focus on what is important to us.

We are realizing that the picture of success painted by the internet and TV isn't always in alignment with the reality we are experiencing in our real lives. As we navigate through life's Transformative Moments, and as we navigate through this Transformative period in our history, we can develop the ability to move through these moments with confidence by knowing what our Unique Strengths are, creating an authentic, crystal-clear Vision we are passionate about, identifying and managing our fears, enrolling others, and developing achievable Goals.

The process of Goal setting allows us to focus and discover whether what we are learning right now is in alignment with our Vision. The process of Goal setting also helps us recognize that there may be things we need to learn in order to achieve our Goals and navigate through Transformative Moments. Goal setting opens us up to the concept of continuous learning, and allows us to make intentional decisions and choices. Some will be right and some will be wrong, but each will feed our need to grow with a sense of purpose.

Goals and Motivation

My Vision from an early age was to play professional baseball because I loved it and happened to be a strong player. My Goal was to win every game, and to win the championship every year. Why was I motivated to win? At the time, I remember that it simply felt good. I learned later in life about how motivation is driven by fear, and understood that my desire to win was probably motivated by a fear of rejection, which is the most common fear for most people.

I received praise and approval for my wins, which made me feel loved and accepted, and…safe. At a very early age we instinctively look for love and acceptance from our parents, guardians and significant influencers. It's what makes us feel safe. If we are loved, we tend to believe that we will continue to be cared for by those who are providing us with a safe environment. If we are rejected, we fear that we will be cast out, forced to fend for ourselves in an unknown and possibly dangerous world. This is why we often find ourselves unconsciously seeking approval, even from people who have no control over our lives.

The need to feel safe is one of our core survival instincts as humans. Often we create a Vision and pursue Goals to satisfy others and in return receive their recognition which makes us feel loved and safe. We see it all the time. We see the daughters of lawyers grow up to be lawyers. We see the sons of engineers grow up to be engineers. These feel like safe decisions to make as we grow up, however these decisions don't always provide us safety or a lasting sense of satisfaction. It has been my experience that when your Unique Strengths, Vision and Goals are in alignment, you will experience a greater sense of safety, confidence, and satisfaction because you are in alignment with your authentic self.

EXERCISE
GOALS

Personal Goals that are designed to move us closer to our Vision give us the confidence to manage our fears and intentionally align with the people who will support our dreams. A Goal is a benchmark that will help you measure your progress toward your Vision. If you are going to Transform with Confidence, you need to set Goals.

This exercise is pretty straightforward. You are going to set Goals that are in alignment with your Vision, and that you can accomplish in the next year. These Goals should be S.M.A.R.T.—Specific, Measurable, Action-oriented, Reasonable and Timely. This exercise will help you further define your Vision.

STEP 1: For each bullet point in your Vision, create a ONE-YEAR Goal. Each Goal should be S.M.A.R.T.

EXAMPLE:

  VISION BULLET POINT: To work at a job I love.

  MOTIVATION: I'll be happy because I'll have a sense of purpose in life.

FEAR TO MANAGE: Fear of Failure

WHY: If I don't find a job I love, I'll be wasting my potential just struggling to get through my day. I'll feel like a failure because I won't be doing anything I feel is meaningful. I've always wanted to make a difference and see the impact of my work.

CRYSTAL CLEAR VISION: I will work at a job where I can use my Unique Strengths, and where I am recognized and appreciated for my talents, energy and creativity. My work space will be open, organized, creative and inspiring. I will work with people I like, and whose Unique Strengths complement my own. I will never be bored, because I will be constantly learning. I will advance in the job quickly and eventually become a leader in my field. I will feel more energized and more satisfied at the end of each day. I will wake up every morning looking forward to my life!

ENROLL WHO: My friend Steve, a recruiter. Ask him what types of jobs hire people whose Unique Strengths are similar to mine.

GOAL: Interview with twelve companies in the next twelve months that hire people with my Unique Strengths, and determine what I need to do to get hired by the company I like the most.

- **Specific? YES**—Interviewing with twelve companies in twelve months that hire people with specific Unique Strengths is **Specific**.
- **Measurable? YES**—Twelve companies in twelve months is **Measurable**.
- **Action-oriented? YES**—The whole Goal is **Action-oriented**.
- **Reasonable? YES**—One interview per month is **Reasonable**.
- **Timely? YES**—Twelve months is **Timely**.

"Take the first step in faith. You don't have to see the whole staircase, just take the first step."
~ Martin Luther King, Jr.

CHAPTER EIGHT

STEPS

Moving to the Next Level

ONE STEP AT A TIME

A Vision is that big picture you see of what life will look like in ten years. It's that picture you're committed to pursuing and are passionate about achieving. Goals are those milestones that tell you if you are on course to achieving your Vision. They are Specific, Measurable, Action-oriented, Reasonable and Timely. Early in life, our Vision and our Goals are greatly influenced by others (parents, teachers, coaches and friends), but through the process of Crystalizing Your Vision, you have come closer to recognizing whether you are pursuing a Vision and Goals that are uniquely yours, or are chasing a Vision that has been defined by somebody else or some other influence.

Taking a Step is critical in the pursuit of a Vision for multiple reasons. If you want to pursue a Vision, you need to actively move toward it. Steps are immediate actions you can take. If you want to be a firefighter, volunteer at the local fire department. If you want to win an Olympic gold in swimming, get in the pool. If you want to own a home, meet with someone who has purchased a home and who would be willing to share the process with you. Steps lead to other Steps. When we take a Step, we learn what the next Step needs to be, and whether we really want to take that next Step.

When we take a Step and it has a positive outcome, we often move onto the next Step with greater enthusiasm and a deeper belief in the Vision we are pursuing. When we take a Step and it has a negative outcome, we need to pause. We need to learn from that moment. What we may learn is that we took the Step incorrectly, or that our Vision needs to be further crystallized and defined, or that it wasn't the right Step. Taking Steps allows us to ensure that our Vision is in alignment with our Unique Strengths and Goals.

A VISION RECONSIDERED

I was in the Seattle airport with Mike, one of my best friends from childhood. We both worked in marketing and sales for different companies and neither of us was passionate about our jobs. Although we both appreciated what we were learning and earning, we were looking for a change. We often talked about opening up a business together and liked to toss ideas back and forth. We had all sorts of ideas for the types of businesses we could run, and particularly liked the idea of working together.

We were headed for Whitefish, Montana, a beautiful town that sits at the base of Big Mountain, twenty minutes from Glacier National Park, one of the most beautiful wilderness settings in the United States. We were meeting two buddies we'd known for years who lived in Whitefish and had opened a pub called The Dire Wolf. It was a local favorite that featured microbrews from around the Northwest and Montana. They served a variety of freshly made soups each day, along with a full menu of lunch and dinner items.

Mike and I landed in Whitefish excited about the prospect of learning more about the pub business. We were thinking of opening a similar kind of pub back in the Portland area. That was our joint Vision at the time. We thought owning a pub would be fun, easy and lucrative.

One of the pub owners, Scott, picked us up at the airport and handed us each a beer as we piled into his truck. (The law at the time allowed passengers in a vehicle to drink.) Of course Scott was not drinking, but the casual vibe appealed to me and Mike. We spent the afternoon with Scott, who good-naturedly answered our many questions about what it was like to own a pub.

The next day we watched Scott work and talked with him more extensively about all the little details of running a restaurant and pub. We looked at his accounting books, and learned how he managed inventory and tracked his food costs and expenses. As the day wore on, both Mike and I started feeling bummed out. This passion of ours to open a pub was getting chipped away as we learned how much work actually goes into running a pub.

On the flight back to Seattle, I was deep in thought when Mike said in a tone that told me what he was thinking, "Well...at least we took the step to learn more about it."

I replied, "You're right... and...I don't think either of us wants to run that type of business. We need to pursue something else."

The truth is that neither of us had the Unique Strengths required to run a pub. Both of us had a Vision of how we wanted to live and enjoy life, but neither of us had set Goals that had anything to do with learning the skills necessary for running a restaurant. I thought to myself, "I don't even know how to cook."

But our trip to Whitefish was not a waste of time. It was a critical learning experience and a Step that we needed to take. Taking that Step caused us to pause and redefine our Vision.

Where Do I Start?

Sammy was a sophomore in college with big hopes of getting into the Merchandise Management Major. In order to get accepted into the Major, she needed to pass math, but it was not her strong suit. She was feeling anxious; she knew that a bad grade in math was going to stand between her and her Goal of getting into the Merchandising Management program, which was a measureable benchmark in achieving her Vision, a career working in fashion and merchandising.

She had six weeks to get her grade up in order to achieve this Goal. This timeline introduced more stress into her life. Whenever we introduce time into the equation, there is an element of stress. In fact, I believe that the only time we feel stress is when we are trying to control time, or when time is controlling us. In spite of her feelings of anxiety, Sammy was passionate about her Vision of working in fashion merchandising, so she decided to take the Steps she needed to reach her Goal.

STEP 1: She asked for help by explaining her situation to a classmate.

STEP 2: Her classmate suggested that she speak with another classmate who knew more about math tutors. Sammy then met with this other classmate and explained her situation.

STEP 3: This classmate suggested a tutor and gave Sammy the tutor's phone number. Sammy called the tutor to explain the situation.

STEP 4: Sammy and the tutor met and the tutor assessed where she needed help and where she didn't.

STEPS 5-13: Sammy continued to meet with this tutor on a weekly basis for the next eight weeks. Each week was an additional Step.

The point of this example is that one Step leads to another Step. This process continues until the Goal is reached. The Goal in this case was getting a good grade in math class so Sammy would be accepted into the Merchandising Management Major.

We can run into trouble when we are thinking Big Steps all the time. Often we confuse Goals with Steps, and we forget that a Step is just a step. We make choices and take Steps every day that are leading us toward our Vision or away from it. Taking Steps removes anxiety. Getting active in the pursuit of our Vision actually removes stress. Taking Steps helps create clarity regarding the next Steps that are needed to achieve the Goal. This clarity creates hope and reinforces our belief that our Vision is possible. The more specific and intentional our Steps become, the more we believe our Vision is not just possible, but probable.

What's the Next Step?

We can get consumed with feeling like we want to move forward but become confused and fearful about how to do it. We don't know what Steps to take. We may even indulge in negative self-talk that can prevent us from taking that first Step. That's why creating and crystallizing a Vision, setting Goals, understanding your Unique Strengths, and managing your fears, before you take Steps is so important. After you have laid the foundation for moving forward toward your Vision, the Steps you need to take become much more clear.

Steps are Immediate Actions you can take in the next 30-90 days toward helping you achieve your one-year Goals. In the process of moving forward you may run into Steps that bring up fear. Managing your fear in order to take action on each Step is important, and understanding the source of that fear is empowering.

Ask yourself:

- Which of your Steps feels scary to you and why?
- Why is one fear stronger than another?
- What moment in your life created this fear?

One way of managing your fear of taking a Step is to ask yourself if there is a Side Step you can take in order to reduce or remove some of that fear. Your Steps don't always have to be Big Steps. Sometimes they can be Micro Steps, like talking to one of the people you have identified on your Vision list, or doing some research on the internet, or taking a class. It could be anything you think will help you achieve your one-year Goal for each bullet point in your Vision. The point is that you need to keep taking Steps. One Step leads to the next.

EXERCISE
TAKING STEPS

STEP 1: For each Goal you came up with in the previous exercise, identify and write down a Step you can take in the next 30-90 days to help you achieve this one-year Goal and ultimately propel you toward your Vision.

EXAMPLE:

VISION BULLET POINT: To work at a job I love.

MOTIVATION: I'll be happy because I'll have a sense of purpose in life.

FEAR TO MANAGE: Fear of Failure

WHY: If I don't find a job I love, I'll be wasting my potential just struggling to get through my day. I'll feel like a failure because I won't be doing anything I feel is meaningful. I've always wanted to make a difference and see the impact of my work.

CRYSTAL CLEAR VISION: I will work at a job where I can use my Unique Strengths, and where I am recognized and appreciated for my talents, energy and creativity. My work space will be open, organized, creative and inspiring. I will work with people I like, and whose Unique Strengths complement my own. I will never be bored, because I will be constantly learning. I will advance in the job quickly and eventually become a leader in my field. I will feel more energized and more satisfied at the end of each day. I will wake up every morning looking forward to my life!

ENROLL WHO: My friend Steve, a recruiter. Ask him what types of jobs hire people whose Unique Strengths are similar to mine.

GOAL: Interview with twelve companies in next twelve months that hire people with my Unique Strengths, and determine what I need to do to get hired by the company I like the most.

STEP: Call Steve this next week to set an appointment to meet for coffee and pick his brain about the types of companies that hire people with my Unique Strengths. Ask him for referrals if appropriate.

Part Two

LESSONS

"It is what it is, but it will become what you make it."

~ Abraham Lincoln

CHAPTER NINE

ACCOUNTABLE OR VICTIM

Life Isn't Fair, or Is It?

IT ISN'T FAIR!
While waiting for my golf buddy in his living room, I found myself watching TV with his three kids (ages five, seven and nine). I noticed these kids watching the commercials with as much interest as they were watching the cartoons. Having been in marketing and sales most of my life, I was intrigued by how the commercials were holding the attention of these kids.

The first commercial was for some cereal like Frosted Flakes. It was an entertaining commercial, and the story and message spoke to these kids. I knew that this cereal company had spent millions of dollars crafting their message to speak specifically to this age group. I also knew how much work they put into their branding and slogans, and even into the little trinkets they stuffed in the cereal boxes. After the cereal commercial was over, one of the kids said, "We need to get that cereal."

I thought to myself, "Wow, they just sold that kid."

The next commercial was for a toy drone, and it had the full attention of these kids. Their enthusiasm went up about ten notches as they saw the kids on the commercial flying the drone around their backyards, over a pool, and at the park.

One of the kids started shouting, "DAD! DAD! DAD.... Come here! Come here!" By the time he got there, the commercial was over, but the kids hadn't forgotten the messages.

Kid One said, "Dad... we need to go to the store and go shopping. There's this cereal I want."

Kid Two said, "Dad... actually... you missed it. They just had a commercial about that drone that Tim got."

Kid Three said, "Yeah... Angie's family got one too, they're awesome."

They all explained the benefits of this toy and what they could do with it and how much fun it would be and so on...I was now thinking to myself that this commercial had these kids selling to their parents.

What do you think their dad said? "No kids... we're not getting you that drone thing. Why don't you go outside and play with the dog..."

Of course the kids' response was "Awww Dad... that isn't fair. Why does Tim get one? Why can't we have one? It's not fair."

I think my friend grumbled something like, "We'll talk about it when I get home."

The kids shouted, "Yay!" like they had already won.

My friend and I got in my car and headed off for the golf course. I said to him, "You know what happens when you get home, don't you?"

He said, "Yeah... they won't forget and we'll need to figure out a way to let them down. I'm not buying that drone thing. It would be broken in a week." He said that what irritated him the most was this concept of "it's not fair."

Where does this concept of fairness come from? The only conclusion I could come to was that even though life isn't fair, somewhere in the process of growing up we are led to believe that it should be fair. I suppose that when we look closely at the marketing and messaging that is hitting us from all angles at every age, we are led to believe that this thing is important or that thing is important, and that without whatever it is, our life is not as good. It's not fair.

My friend said that he and his wife would have to sit down with their kids and teach them that life is not fair, that they are not going to get everything they want, and if they do really want something, then they're going to have to work for it, and they are going to have to create a plan to make it happen.

To transform as an individual, a society, or a world, we need to be accountable for ourselves and let go of the idea that life owes us anything, or that we must have what someone else has. If we are really going to transform as a society, we will need to heighten our awareness of the messaging hitting us, and what it's leading us to believe about ourselves, about others, and about the world we live in. When your Vision is clear and your Goals and Steps are well outlined, you will be better able to recognize whether what is being sold or marketed to you is in alignment with helping you achieve your Vision.

Why Me?

I was headed into my sophomore year in college and excited about the upcoming baseball season. The year before I was undefeated as a pitcher, but only had a few opportunities to pitch as we had a very strong group of pitchers among the upper classmen on our varsity team. Several of them had been drafted and were headed off to play professional baseball, so my sophomore year was going to be a great opportunity for me to move into the starting lineup on a regular basis.

I had just started fall baseball practice when I got a call from my dad saying that he and my mom were getting a divorce. I played it off as no big deal, but inside it really hurt. We'd always celebrated holidays and birthdays as a family, and we'd always had lots of fun. All of that was now gone. Both my parents called me regularly to see if I was okay, but I had no interest in talking to either of them.

They'd rocked my world as I knew it. By all definitions, this was a Transformative Moment in my life and I was left to figure out how I was going to handle it moving forward.

My grades started suffering, I was spending too many nights out on the town with friends and too many nights doing nothing but just feeling sorry for myself. Worse yet, this distraction was affecting my pitching. I couldn't focus and was struggling to throw strikes. That struggle continued right up to the start of the season. As the bus pulled away with all of the players on the team except me, I remember feeling really sorry for myself. They were headed down south for the spring road trip and would be gone for a week, while I was left to play a couple of junior varsity games with a bunch of freshmen.

I was going to start the first JV game of my entire life while the team I should have been on was about to play the season opener in sunny California. I had a good warm up session in the bull pen and felt confident about the way I was throwing. I remember walking down to the dugout from the bullpen to get ready for the first inning. We had fifteen minutes to go until game time. I sat in that dugout and looked around at our team and the team we were about to play. I remember saying out loud, "What am I doing here?"

One of the JV teammates said, "What do you mean? You're the starting pitcher."

I said, "I know... don't worry about it," but I was thinking, "Why in the hell am I playing baseball with the JV team? I don't belong on this team. I belong on the varsity team."

Playing on the JV team had nothing to do with my Goals, my Vision or my Unique Strength. I asked myself, "What can I do about this?" I told myself that I had to quit feeling sorry for myself. I realized in that moment that feeling sorry for myself wasn't getting me anywhere, and that I needed to take positive steps to get back to where I felt I should be.

I looked at the other team and thought, "This is my game today!" I talked to myself throughout the entire game, "This game is mine. I own it." I had my focus back. I was taking ownership of my outcome. I threw a one-hitter that day with full control of my pitches and felt like I had rediscovered myself. I was good enough to get elevated back to the varsity team by the following week, which led to a very successful season.

I think about this story whenever I start to feel a little sorry for myself. What I realize now is that I was allowing myself to be a victim of circumstance. I know now that I don't have control over others, but I do have a choice as to how I respond or react to the moments that come up in life. I was choosing to feel sorry for myself, which was preventing me from pursuing my Vision and Goals with confidence and focus. At the time, I didn't have the awareness to manage this Transformative Moment, so that I could Transform with Confidence.

ACCOUNTABILITY MATTERS

Personal accountability matters. Integrity, trustworthiness, honesty, reliability, and transparency all matter. To understand what it means to be accountable, you must first understand what it really means to be a victim. No one enjoys being the victim. Yet, many of us allow ourselves to play the victim, or we embrace victim behaviors. Why do we do this? Because it's sometimes easier to play the victim than it is to take responsibility for our situation. It's easy to give up. It takes no talent, and sometimes it even gets us attention.

The reality is that you may very well have been victimized during your life as a result of the circumstances into which you were born, or you may have been a victim of a situation over which you had no control at the time. But this does not mean that you have to be the victim for the rest of your life. If you really want to achieve your Vision and get through a Transformative Moment, you're going to have to move past the behaviors associated with being a victim. You are going to have to start to take some personally accountable steps wherever you can.

If you're handicapped somehow—circumstantially, financially, physically, emotionally—you may have to go about achieving your Vision a little differently than somebody who is more advantaged or from a more privileged, comfortable, stable or safe environment. We see people all the time who have transcended serious injuries or moved beyond painful, even debilitating incidents by marshalling the courage to move beyond their circumstances in order to accomplish their Goals and pursue their Vision.

By looking at moments as moments, and by recognizing that a certain moment, or series of moments, or even an entire period of time, may have been profoundly transformative, and may even have had a negative impact on your life, you can begin to consciously choose which moments you want to allow to have a lasting impact on your identity and behavior. Regardless of your circumstances, the first step toward accountability is painting a Vision of what you want your life to look like.

Even if you feel your resources are limited, your Vision is just as achievable as anyone else's, as long as you believe it is, and as long as you are willing to take the Steps necessary to make it happen. You may have more Steps to go through than someone else, but achieving your Vision really boils down to how badly you want it and whether you are willing to go through the necessary process to get there. Life isn't fair and some of us will need to take more

Steps than others, but true accountability is empowering, enlightening and energizing. It takes perseverance. It takes a focus. It takes a belief that you're going to achieve the Vision you've outlined for yourself.

True accountability also allows you the opportunity to enjoy each moment in the process. Every Step, every moment, is an opportunity to learn something. When you accept the fact that you are who you are based on every moment, influence and experience up to the current moment, then you can reasonably accept the fact that you will become who you will be in the future based on how you look at and define every moment you encounter going forward.

From every moment in the past, you have learned something. You need to embrace the fact that continuous learning is woven into the fabric of life, whether you want it to be or not. And, when you embrace the concept of continuous learning, you will find yourself displaying victim behaviors far less frequently, because you will choose to learn how to apply any knowledge gained toward pursuing your Vision.

The Oz Principle, a book written by Roger Connors, Tom Smith and Craig Hickman, does a very good job of outlining the steps to accountability. It starts by identifying six victim behaviors:

1. Finger pointing—"So and so did that. Wasn't me."
2. Wait and see—"Let someone else take care of it."
3. It's not my fault—"Don't look at me."
4. Cover your tail—"Well, that's not what I wanted to do."
5. Ignore, deny, lie—These are obvious.
6. Acting confused—"I didn't know what you meant by that."

Then it outlines **Steps to Accountability:**

1. See there is a Problem
2. Take Ownership of the Problem
3. Solve It
4. Do It

These steps seem logical and straightforward. The challenge is applying them consistently. The good news is you don't need to do all the work yourself, or solve the problem all by yourself. You just need to take ownership of the problem and enroll others to help you solve it. If it's truly a problem, if it's truly a Transformative Moment, you can't ignore it, you can't let others just take care of it, and you can't make excuses. You need to own the moment.

Remember, you cannot always control everything that comes into your life or how everything will actually manifest, but you always have 100% control over how you choose to react to it. You can choose to be a victim, or you can choose to be accountable and open to what is possible. You can choose to be solution-focused. Being a Victim is a choice. Being Accountable is a choice. Pursuing your Vision is a choice, and it requires accountability.

A Recap of the Work You've Done So Far

1. You have established your "Unique Strengths" with the help of others. These are those strengths that come naturally to you and actually give you energy—your strengths above all other strengths.
2. You've learned about the "Four Stages of Learning"—you're always in one of these stages. Life will present you with something to learn every day.
3. You've been introduced to the "Laws of Attraction"—Perceive, Believe, and Achieve.
4. You've written out and crystallized the Vision of what your life will look like in five to ten years.
5. You've designed Goals by which you will be able to measure your progress.

6. You've synthesized Steps to achieving these Goals and ultimately your Vision.
7. You've identified people with whom you can connect to help you achieve your Vision.
8. You've received some insight into how the brain works and makes decisions. We all have a core instinct to feel safe.
9. You've connected with a better understanding of how to recognize fears and motivators.
10. You know how to quickly identify your own fears.
11. You've gotten a better understanding of "Why" and why it's so important.
12. You understand the concept of staying open to what is possible.

The hardest part of formulating and committing to a Vision is truly believing—at your core—that it is achievable. Wishful thinking doesn't work if you really want your Vision to come true. It needs to be a Vision for which you are 100% accountable.

EXERCISE
ACCOUNTABILITY

STEP 1: Write down five instances in which you have chosen to be a victim. These could be situations where you knew you needed some help but were afraid to ask for it. That's a common victim behavior. These could be moments when you felt something wasn't fair, or moments when you knew there was a problem but ignored it. These could be situations in which you felt that what was going on was out of your control.

STEP 2: Reread the five instances you wrote down. Take some time and ask yourself... "What could I have done differently to have been able to avoid being the victim in that situation? What could I have done to have been accountable?" Look back at all the steps that led up to the situation or moment. What could you have done differently? What have you learned?

STEP 3: Now...throw that list away! It's in the past. Be grateful for what you have learned and keep moving forward.

"Every choice you make has an end result."

~ ZIG ZIGLAR

CHAPTER TEN

YOU CHOOSE YOUR "ACCIDENT"

Co-creating the Life You Want

THE DEVIL WENT DOWN TO GEORGIA

When I was about ten, my mom informed me that I was going to learn how to play an instrument. At that time, all I thought about was shooting hoops and playing football in the backyard with my friends. That was the best! But, if I had to learn to play an instrument, I wanted to play the fiddle. I wanted to be able to play "The Devil Went Down to Georgia" like Charlie Daniels. I had heard it over at a friend's house and liked the song. Off to violin class I went thinking I was going to "crush it."

Little did I know that in order to play the violin or fiddle (I wasn't sure what the difference was, but "fiddle" sounded cooler to me), I would need to practice a lot. The first class was about how to hold the fiddle. There was actually a lot to this. After three classes and about one hour of practice a day, I could barely scratch out the song, "Hot Cross Buns." To add insult to injury, while I was practicing, I could see out the living room window that my friends were happily playing football in the street. I was practicing the fiddle to fulfill my mom's Vision, but all I wanted was to be outside playing ball with my friends.

After three weeks, I was nowhere near being able to play like Charlie Daniels, and nowhere near playing "The Devil Went Down to Georgia," so I made the choice to quit. This was not my Vision. This was not going to be my future. I was passionate about playing sports; that was going to be my future. I made the choice to spend more time doing what my Unique Strengths led me to do, which also happened to be what I actually enjoyed doing. It filled me with energy to be doing what I was passionate about.

This story is important for two reasons. As adults, we need to allow our children to explore and discover their Unique Strengths. We also need to be aware of the choices we make that will have a lasting influence on them, and pay attention to the choices they will ultimately pass along to the next generations. As children, we make choices based on the influences of our parents, other adults, and peers as well as our own personal experiences and interests. As we grow older and are inundated with ever more information, we need to pause and think about why we are making the choices we are making to begin with, before making the choices that lead us to action and toward, or away from, our Vision.

- Which influences are having an impact on the choices we are making?
- Are we making choices that are in alignment with our Vision?
- Are the choices we're making in alignment with the next Steps we need to be taking in order to achieve our Vision and navigate ourselves through Transformative Moments?

Turkey Dip or Reuben?

Okay... not all choices are big choices, and not all choices have to do with achieving your ultimate Vision. I was out for lunch with a friend at a local pub, a perfect place to spend an afternoon hanging out and talking while the raindrops fell outside. My friend and I slow sipped our IPAs and talked until the waiter asked us what he could get us to eat. My friend said, "I think we need to look at the menus, can you come back in a few minutes."

The waiter said, "No problem, take your time... I'll be back in a minute."

As my friend and I perused the menu, I told him that a business associate had once told me, "Never make a decision until you have to...and, you need to decide what you really want first, prior to making the decision." With these bits of wisdom in mind, I said to my friend, "Put the menu down. Let's try something new.... Let's explain to the waiter what we feel like eating and how we want to feel after we eat."

My friend said, "Sure... let's do it."

I was thinking that we would describe our immediate "Vision" to the waiter, enroll him, and then let him guide us in our choice of food. We just had to manage the fear of looking odd in this situation.

A few minutes later, the waiter returned. Since it was my idea—and to help my buddy understand what I had in mind—I went first. The waiter asked if we were ready to order, and I said, "We're going to need your help."

The waiter said, "Sure."

I said, "Okay... here's what I feel like eating. I'd like a sandwich of some kind, but I'd like something that's kind of like a Reuben but also kind of like a French Dip without roast beef. I'd like to feel only medium full after eating, so I have room for one more IPA after lunch."

The waiter paused for a moment and said, "Hmm... What I think we could do is take our turkey sandwich with the pickled relish, remove the relish, grill the sandwich with some Swiss cheese and serve it au jus."

I said, "Brilliant! Let's do it."

My buddy then said, "I'd like something kind of crunchy like a taco, but hearty...something that will make me feel warm afterwards...I'm feeling cold."

The waiter laughed and said, "Let me think about that one." He then asked, "Do you like soup?"

My buddy said, "Yes... what kind of soup do you have in mind?"

The waiter said, "We make a great beer potato cheese soup and I can have the cook include bits of the crispy pita chips we use with our hummus appetizer."

My friend said, "Sounds good... let's go for it."

The waiter left and we both looked at each other and laughed. I wondered what the cook would say when the waiter got to the kitchen with our order.

Just a little bit later, we both got our meals and they were amazing. The waiter told us that the cook enjoyed the challenge of concocting our meals. He went on to say that more people should order the way we did, because it was fun.

We learned five important things that day:

1. We didn't have to make a choice off the menu.
2. We don't need to make every decision ourselves.
3. When we enrolled someone else in our Vision, the choice became easier.
4. Others want to help you achieve your Vision if they understand it.
5. It was a win-win for everyone: us, the waiter and the cook.

The choices we make don't always have to be made the way we've been taught they need to be made. Sometimes, we need to let others guide us in making our choices, and sometimes we need to simply not make a choice until it's necessary to do so. The internet, marketers, and institutions around the world are bombarding us with information. We are being conditioned to make choices at a very rapid pace, and often they are choices we are not ready to make, or even prepared to make. This can create some level of anxiety because we feel we are not in control.

The power of choice is an important gift we have been given. Every day, we make thousands of choices consciously and subconsciously. Some are big, some are small, some are scary and some are easy. When we are hyper-focused on our Vision and willing to pursue the Steps required to reach that Vision, we find that our choices become easier to make, and will enhance our confidence in meeting Transformative Moments head on and navigating them with peace and certainty.

MID-CHAPTER EXERCISE
CHOICE

STEP 1: Write down five times you made a bad choice, or five regrets you have. Read your list once

STEP 2: Throw that list away. Let that stuff go. To achieve a Vision, you need to forgive yourself, forgive others, and move on.

STEP 3: Make some new choices. Write down five behaviors you can change that will help you achieve your Vision.

STEP 4: Read them often. Practice them daily.

Accident Investigation

I was sitting in Accident Investigation, a class I was taking to fill an elective for my college degree. I thought it might be an easy class to take during the baseball season and it seemed like it might be interesting with puzzles to figure out and problem solving.

Our professor was a young guy who exuded confidence named Anthony Veltri. Right away, he challenged the class by asking, "Did you know there is no such thing as an accident? Every accident could have been prevented. Can anybody name an accident that couldn't have been prevented?" Immediately, twenty hands went up and he called on the first student.

The student said, "A car accident."

Veltri asked the student, "What time of day did the car accident you're talking about take place?"

The student said, "Let's say 5pm, in rush hour traffic...and the car was rear ended."

Veltri then asked the student a series of questions:

- Could the driver have left five minutes later than he did?
- Could the driver have left five minutes earlier than he did?
- Could the driver have not gone to work that day?
- Could the driver have called in sick that day?

- Could the other driver have left five minutes earlier or later?
- Could either driver have taken an alternate route that day?
- Could either driver have taken public transportation instead of driving?
- Could either of them have taken another job in another part of the city?

You could very quickly see where this line of questioning was going. Veltri was simply pointing out that there is always a series of events or <u>choices</u> that lead up to the event that we define as an accident.

The class turned into a lively debate as one student after another tried to think of something that would break Veltri's model:

- A waiter spilling the drinks.
- A shark attack.
- Finding a suitcase full of money.

Each time, Veltri would ask, "Were there a series of choices or events that led up to this accident?"

Each time, someone else in the class would say, "Well yes." And they would point out some steps, moments, or choices that led up to that "accident."

- The waiter could have walked slower or carried fewer drinks.
- The shark attack victim could have not gone swimming that day.
- Finding a suitcase full of money would not have happened if the person had not taken a walk that day.

Veltri's model held true no matter what. Many of the students thought it was ridiculous, but you couldn't beat it. He told us that some of the other professors in the college were not fans of his model. I thought that perhaps that was because it challenged conventional definitions.

I've been a witness to many events and moments that most people would classify as accidents. Every time, I ask myself, is there anything that could have prevented this accident from occurring? Were there any choices made (conscious or unconscious) that led up to this event? The answer is always yes.

There is always a series of events, moments and <u>choices</u> that lead us to where we are right now. It's a big concept to wrap your mind around. When you start to think that nothing has ever happened by accident and everything going forward will never be an accident, it changes the way you approach your life. There will always be a series of events, moments, experiences, and choices that will lead to any eventual event, incident or "accident."

The point of this section on "accidents" is not to open a debate about whether or not accidents exist. Unexpected things will always be a part of life. The point of this section is to give you a different perspective as well as a way to think about and deal with the choices you make and any unexpected moments that may come about in your future.

When an accident does happen, pause and look at it closely. Were there a series of events that led up to this moment (accident)? You will always find that there were. What can you learn from this accident? When you choose to pursue a Vision, pause and look at your Steps closely. Are the Steps you are planning to take going to lead you to more unexpected positive moments—happy accidents—or unexpected negative moments—unhappy accidents? Sometimes you can't know the answer until you take a few Steps, but when you recognize that there is no such thing as an accident, you will be better able to manage your behaviors in a personally accountable way. You will also tend to experience far fewer situations in which you feel victimized, or lapse into victim behaviors.

Our Happy Accident

My daughter wanted a dog, specifically a yellow Lab. My wife and I had a Vision of being able to pick out a puppy from a litter and have that moment be a life experience for our daughter. We found a breeder south of Portland, but when we drove there, we discovered that it was a major breeding operation. They were breeding Labs for hunting and were charging $1000-$2000 for a puppy. We had not planned to spend that much money on a dog; we just wanted a family pet.

The whole thing turned us off, and we left feeling disappointed. Nonetheless, we continued to hold a very clear Vision of what we wanted. On the ride home we got a call from a friend who had recently gotten a black Lab. We told him about how we were looking for a Lab, and how the breeder we'd just seen was not right for us. Our friend suggested that we check out another smaller breeder who happened to be closer to our house.

We swung by on the way home and it ended up that all the dogs there were being bred from the same bloodlines the expensive hunting Labs were from. We ended up paying $200 for a Lab puppy, but most importantly we got to sit down with our daughter in an old barn where we were surrounded by a dozen little puppies and allow our puppy to pick us.

The importance of enrolling others isn't just about getting support. It's about marshalling the "higher power" that we're all a part of through our connections with other human beings. If my friend hadn't called me at that moment (a happy accident), and if we hadn't taken the Step to visit one more breeder, we wouldn't have been driving home with our puppy, Raleigh, the same day we went out looking.

Higher Power

My personal belief is that there is a "higher power" or a higher energy that we're all part of. From the beginning of time human beings have been trying to understand and define it. We've called it God, Spirit, Angels, the Universe...many different names depending on our religious or spiritual orientation. I believe we tap into this higher power when we practice the Steps we've identified as the actions we must take on our path toward the realization of our Vision. In this pursuit, we develop a stronger appreciation for every Step we take and every lesson we learn along the way and we find that our higher power (regardless of what we each define as our higher power), actually wants us to succeed in attaining the Vision we've committed to.

The way I look at it is, if you understand what your Unique Strengths are, you're going to put yourself in situations in which you can capitalize on those Unique Strengths. If your Vision is clear, and you manage your fears, if you create Goals and Steps that serve your Vision, you will access this higher power more easily and directly, which is how happy accidents or "synchronicities" occur. Some would call this the "Law of Attraction."

The happy or unhappy "accidents" that occur in your life are there to either remind you that you're on the right track toward your Vision, or give you the awareness that something you're doing needs to change. If you inadvertently create an unhappy accident, you have the opportunity to take accountability for it, and then leverage what you've learned going forward. It may be that you need to alter your Vision slightly or consider the possibility that your Vision is out of alignment with your Unique Strengths, or that your Goals or Steps need to be tweaked. Learning and growing are inevitable, but you always have the option to take full accountability for your opportunity to learn by looking for the lessons and determining how you might do it differently, or exactly the same way, next time.

When you take accountability, your choices are going to be more conscious, they're going to have more impact, and more power. You're going to be able to create the synchronicities you want and attract the life you want if you're willing to face yourself and manage your fears. From a victim or fear-based place you never create what you want. You only create more of what you don't want.

EXERCISE
THERE ARE NO ACCIDENTS

There are always stages of learning regardless of where you are in your life. Becoming personally accountable requires that you manage your fears and recognize that the current moment you're in is an opportunity to learn something. An accountable behavior might be asking yourself, "What am I supposed to be learning from this moment right now?"

STEP 1: Make a list of three unhappy "accidents" you've experienced recently, like tripping and twisting your ankle, getting an unexpected bad grade, or being rear-ended. Then list three happy "accidents" you've experienced recently, like getting an unexpected raise, meeting a new love, or winning a prize.

STEP 2: Write down the series of events or steps that led up to the negative and positive moments you perceived as accidents.

STEP 3: What could you have done differently to avoid the negative situations from occurring? What did you do to create the positive situations?

STEP 4: What did you learn from these "accidents" and from this exercise that will serve you in the future?

"It's a funny thing. The more I practice, the luckier I get."

~ Arnold Palmer

CHAPTER ELEVEN

PRACTICE AND FOCUS

Discipline Will Set You Free!

DO IT WELL...OR NOT AT ALL

I grew up in the suburbs of Portland, Oregon in an area called Raleigh Hills. It was a peaceful neighborhood with lots of open space. We lived on about an acre of land, and as much as I loved having such a big backyard, I also hated it. Every week from March through October, the grass needed to be mowed, and the spring rains that inundated Oregon didn't make it easy. The grass was often wet and seemed like it grew about a foot a week.

One weekend when I was around twelve, I was informed that it was my turn to mow the lawn. I headed out to the yard with a bit of an attitude because I'd just had to tell my friends that I couldn't play hoops with them until I was finished with the lawn, which took about two hours to mow. That meant I would have less time on my Saturday for playing with my friends. I felt it was unfair that I was stuck mowing the lawn when I could have been having fun doing what I really wanted to do.

I set about mowing the wet lawn and it was taking forever. The grass was so wet that the clippings were sticking in clumps to the wheels of the mower and leaving a thick trail as I made my way back and forth across the lawn. I didn't care. I just wanted to get the job done so I could go play with my friends. To make the task even more onerous, the clippings pile was at the back of the yard, and because the grass was so long, I was having to take twice as many trips with the wheelbarrow to dump the grass that was accumulating in the grass catcher behind the mower.

I knew the job I was doing was not my best effort, but I was really hoping my dad wouldn't give me a hard time about it. When I was done, I washed off the mower, stuck it in the garage, and went inside to clean up. I told my dad I was heading over to my friend's house to shoot some hoops.

He said, "Before you go, let's take a look at the lawn." I knew instantly that this wasn't going to go well. We headed out the back door and walked around the yard.

My dad said, "Jeff, you know the saying… 'Once you have a job begun, never leave it till it's done. Be the labor great or small. Do it well or not at all.'" My dad pulled the rake out of the garage and said, "Let's get all the grass clippings that fell outside of the mower raked up."

"Arghhhh!!!"

Mowing an acre of grass every week was certainly not one of my Vision bullet points, but learning the value of a strong work ethic has stayed with me. Pursuing a Vision takes hard work and a strong work ethic. It takes **practice** and it takes **focus**. You have to work at making your Vision a reality, and you have to work to get through a Transformative Moment.

10,000 Hours of Practice Makes Perfect

Malcom Gladwell writes in his book, *Outliers: The Story of Success,* about the idea that 10,000 hours of "deliberate practice" is required in order to become an expert in a particular field. How does one even conceive of 10,000 hours? If the average work week is forty hours, and if you work fifty weeks in a year, you will have worked 2,000 hours at the end of one year. So, in five years, working at that rate, you will have worked 10,000 hours.

I'm reminded of this when I watch professional athletes like golf pro, Tiger Woods, basketball star, Stephen Curry, Olympic swimmer, Katie Ledecky, and tennis champion, Serena Williams. When we see these sports stars on TV they are almost always shown in competition. We rarely, if ever, see their practice routines televised. But, if you were to look at how many hours they practice, you would quickly realize that these people have all put well beyond 10,000 hours of practice into honing their Unique Strengths in service to achieving their Visions.

Look at the most successful folks in the world. They have put countless hours into whatever their craft/art/profession/passion might be. Aside from the number of hours they spend practicing their skills, the one thing they all have in common is that they started with a Unique Strength they developed somewhere along the way. They chose a Vision they were passionate about, and utilized their Unique Strength in the pursuit of that Vision.

Tele-What?

I was leading a sales training seminar for a group of young professionals who were interested in pursuing careers in sales and marketing, and believed that this career path would provide them with the sort of lifestyle and income they desired. They had all been out of school a few years and had worked in positions that required client communication and some level of customer service and support. They all said they "loved people, were good communicators and good at sales."

I started the workshop by asking them a simple question: "How many of you love getting telemarketing calls?" Nobody raised a hand. I asked them why, and got a lot of responses that had to do with telemarketers being pushy, aggressive, rude, and inconsiderate. I asked them if they had ever received a call that actually went well. Almost all of the hands went up.

We talked about the difference between good sales people and not-so-good sales people, and how obvious it was when you encountered a real professional. I asked the group what qualities they thought made a successful salesperson. The group said that successful salespeople are not pushy, that they ask good questions and listen well. They are educated, know how to solve problems, and are in control of the conversation. They also recognize when things are not a fit.

"How often do you encounter a salesperson like this?" I asked. Most everyone agreed that it was about 1 in 10 or about 10%. Some said it was maybe even 1 in a 100, or about 1%. There is a lot more that goes into being a good salesperson, but the point of this story is that only about 10% reach the level where others see them as a "pro." They are the 10% who have put countless hours into getting better.

Imagine entering a number into the phone fifty times a day to make a telemarketing call. Then imagine doing this 261 working days a year. That is 13,050 telemarketing calls in a year, and if you're fortunate, you'll connect with about 10% of the people you call. From a salesperson's perspective this is exhausting, and because of this, many give up on sales early in their careers. They don't give themselves the time it takes to hone their craft. It is hard work, and requires real perseverance and the ability to handle rejection. It takes practice to become a pro.

When do you really become a pro at something? You will start to recognize it when the game slows down for you, when you can literally see how things are going to unfold before they unfold. You've put in the time. Look at the strongest leaders in any company; they are not reactionary. They are proactive, they take the Steps necessary to move forward toward their Goals and Vision. They lean on the experience they have gained from their years of practice, and they rely on the experience and expertise of others.

To chase a Vision and achieve it, you need to practice. Practice your Unique Strength, practice managing your fears, practice enrolling others, practice setting Goals and taking Steps. Giving up takes no talent. Pursuing a Vision takes practice and hard work.

But...I Really, Really Want It!!

Great! Go make it happen! That's what I tell people all the time. I've never questioned whether a person really wants something. I believe that most people who say they really want something, really do want what they want. What I question is whether they are willing to put in the time, and whether they have the focus and a process to make it happen. I also ask, when something goes a little sideways (a Transformative Moment), if they have the willingness to learn from it, and the ability to regain focus and continue forward toward their Vision.

Achieving a Vision and managing a Transformative Moment takes focus as well as hard work. It takes that undying belief that you are going to achieve your Vision, and the willingness to do the work necessary to get there. Your Goals and Steps are the "how to make it happen." Achieving them requires focus and practice. Some of the bullet points in your Vision will be easy to achieve. Some will not be.

When you focus on your Goals and Vision and practice your Unique Strength and all the other skills you will need to move forward, you will accomplish the little Steps that lead to your larger Goals along your journey toward your Vision. As a result of persevering in your practice, your Vision will become increasingly clear, and your confidence that you can get through Transformative Moments will significantly expand.

It's a choice to focus, and it takes practice to focus. It is also so much easier to focus when you are pursuing a Vision you are passionate about. If you are struggling with focus, revisit the exercises. Part of achieving your Vision is leveraging your Unique Strengths and enrolling those who can help. When doing so, you will see how each moment is either leading you toward or away from your Vision. Without focus, your Vision and Goals are unattainable. Concentrate on them, believe they will happen and focus on doing the things you need to do to make them happen.

Awww...Man...Don't Should On Me

How can we maintain our focus? A wise person once told me, "Don't let people 'should' on you, and make sure you never 'should' on someone else." Pay attention to the words that come out of your mouth, as well as the words you spend time listening to. As you engage with others, take the time to ask them questions in order to understand what kind of help they may need from you.

Pay attention to the questions they ask you. Are they sincerely interested in supporting you and your Vision, or do they have an agenda that doesn't align with your needs? Lead others to discover for themselves what they should or should not do. And conversely, pay attention to whether you are being given the opportunity to discover for yourself what you should or should not do, or are being told which direction to take.

I have caught myself "shoulding" on my daughter many times. I think it's natural for a parent or a grandparent to feel like they need to share their thoughts from time to time. Often, it is in the best interest of the child, but keep in mind that information is now hitting young adults and all of us at a faster rate than at any time in the history of this world. What someone "should" do or "should" have done, according to the values and/or protocol from some other time in history, isn't always applicable any more.

Avoid the Dream Stealers

Why is it so important to have a crystal clear Vision? It's your rock. It helps you focus. It helps you understand what you need to practice in order to achieve it. When you share your Vision with other people, which is a necessary step in transforming with confidence, you will find that most people want to help. When you talk to people who have gone on to reach "pro" status or have achieved their Visions, you usually hear that there were people in their corner cheering them on in the pursuit of their Vision.

On the other hand, you will also occasionally hear that these people were exposed to "dream stealers" along the way. People who challenged their Vision or tried to knock them off course somehow. Beware of dream stealers. Look out for words and phrases like:

- "You can't do that..."
- "That's impossible..."
- "How are you ever going to be able to do that?"

- "What are you thinking?"
- "What you should do is…"

Why do people dream steal? Often it's unintentional. It's a learned behavior that some people don't even realize they are engaging in. Other times, people are covering up their own insecurities or fears. If you feel you are possibly in the presence of a dream stealer, the questions to ask yourself are: "Is your dream or Vision being challenged in a positive manner, and are the questions you are being asked helping you learn more and helping you crystallize your Vision, or are they simply criticizing it somehow?" Having an awareness of what a dream stealer is, will allow you to protect your Vision.

You don't have to enroll everyone in your Vision, but you will have to actively enroll those who can provide support or be of assistance in some productive way. You can choose to put yourself in situations that will help you move forward toward your Vision, or in situations that may derail you from your dreams. It's up to you! Protect your dreams. Don't let others steal them.

EXERCISE
PRACTICE AND FOCUS

STEP 1: Write down five habits or behaviors you can change to help increase your focus. Write down five lessons you learned from something that didn't go right.

STEP 2: Write down five things you have spent over 10,000 hours of practice on. Or... those things you have spent the most time on. Write them in order and just estimate the hours.

STEP 3: Take some time and consider how the things you have spent the most hours practicing have contributed to your Unique Strengths, and how you might leverage those Strengths in your next Steps toward pursuing your Vision.

"The present moment is all you ever have."

~ Eckhart Tolle

Chapter Twelve

APPRECIATING THE MOMENT

Paying Attention Pays Off

THE POWER OF A SHOWER

I had the opportunity to attend a conference in Silicon Valley called Wisdom 2.0. I didn't really know what to expect, but the lineup of speakers was amazing. Senior executives, founders and owners from Google, Facebook, eBay, and more, as well as the Dalai Lama via Skype, and Eckhart Tolle, the author of *The Power of Now: A Guide to Spiritual Enlightenment*. This wasn't a conference dedicated to selling, marketing, or how to make more money; it was a conference about being mindful about the work we do on the internet.

The last speaker of the day ended up being Eckhart Tolle, who led us (300+ attendees) through a meditation in which we were asked to focus on being in the moment. Tolle spoke about what it means to be present and gave us some exercises to try. He described how learning to focus on the sensation of a single drop of water when you're in the shower is an effective way to clear the mind and come into a state of peace before a day of work. I was thinking to myself that a shower shoots out a ton of water, and it comes out in a stream, not one drop at a time. However, I grew up in rainy Oregon, and I knew what one drop felt like. It was that first big drop that hit you before the skies opened up.

When I was back in my hotel room after the conference was over, I jumped in the shower to get ready for dinner, and decided to challenge myself. Could I focus on feeling just one drop of water at a time? In that shower I had an amazing insight into what it means to really clear your mind, and how difficult it can be. The entire time I was in the shower, that little voice in my head kept saying, "Did you feel just one drop? Try again... concentrate." It was incredibly difficult to focus on just one drop of water hitting my head. I found my thoughts going back to the events of the day and anticipating the evening ahead. Nonetheless, even though it was hard to focus on feeling only one drop, I found that an amazing sense of calm came over me in my quest.

For the next five years, every time I got in the shower in the morning, I practiced this exercise. The practice strengthened my ability to be more aware and more appreciative of each moment. I found that I became much less reactionary and much more calm in the daily pursuit of my Vision. I had more awareness of what was going on around me, and how it could either help me move toward my Vision, or derail me in some way.

It started with the power of the shower and then transformed into a ten minute daily meditation during which I would sit somewhere and focus only on what was happening before me. Some days, I sat on a bench in the park. Other days, I sat at a little league baseball game, or in front of a fire in my backyard fire pit. It's not often in today's busy world that we make the time to just be still and enjoy the moment.

In the process of doing this, I gained an appreciation for the moments I was experiencing and a heightened awareness of which moments were leading me toward my Vision, which moments were a rest stop on the journey, or which were simply knocking me off course. What I also grew to realize is that in every moment, there was something I could learn, as these moments allowed me to really focus on the next Steps I was going to need to take in pursuit of my Vision. The calmness I experienced by practicing just being in the moment, created clarity around these Steps and allowed for a deeper sense of gratitude and the ability to discover what I may have been missing while moving too quickly.

Being Present—Living in the Moment

Thought leader Dan Sullivan suggests that there are three ways people measure themselves. It goes something like this:

1. The Gap: Measuring where you are now versus where you want to be in the future. A frustration can develop when constantly measuring the present against where you think you want to be or "should" be.
2. The Other Gap: Measuring where you are now versus where you were in the past. Blaming your current circumstances on the events that occurred throughout your past. A kind of Victim behavior.
3. The Present: Measuring yourself right now. Understanding there is a past which has helped you become who you are, and acknowledging that though you have a Vision, you are completely focused on enjoying the process and where you are right now.

It's a natural tendency to go back and forth—measuring our current position against where we were in the past, and then measuring our current position in relation to the future we wish to inhabit. Use the past and future to help you be accountable for what you need to do right NOW. Life is a process, and when we understand this, we start to appreciate that every moment in the process matters. It's okay to have a Vision and Goals, but it's important to understand that you need to be "present" in order for them to manifest.

Believe It, Achieve it!

When your Vision is solid and your Goals are defined you will find that you will attract into your life the things you need when you need them. You can't always dictate exactly how things, situations, or people will manifest, or exactly when they will come into your life. Earlier in this book, I shared a quote from Napoleon Hill's famous book, *Think and Grow Rich,* and it's worth repeating: "Whatever the mind can conceive and believe, it can achieve."

The tricky one is "believing" because our beliefs are based on all of our influences and experiences up to the present moment. The lessons in this book are designed to help you SEE your Goals and the Steps you need to take so that you can SEE your path forward and thus build a stronger BELIEF that you will actually ACHIEVE your Vision. Your belief in your ability to achieve your Vision is what will propel you through Transformative Moments.

Understand this, and you will look at each moment a little bit differently. You will understand that every moment is happening for a reason, and that by being present in the moment, you will become more aware of the choices that lead you to particular moments. And, this awareness gives you the ability to be accountable for your choices moving forward. There is no such thing as an accident. Focus on the negative and guess what, more negative enters your life. Focus on the positive and you get more positive. Focus on your Vision, and you are more likely to achieve it. Your actions follow your thoughts, and your thoughts determine your results.

We're Not Cookie-Cutter Anymore

By the time you reach this part of the book, you have started the journey toward crystallizing your Vision, and you have also realized, if you hadn't previously, that you are completely unique. There is no other person just like you. There never will be. You have had a unique set of circumstances that define your life. When you consider this, comparing yourself to anyone else becomes a fruitless exercise. It's impossible to ever be the same as someone else.

However, learning from others and learning about the Steps others have taken to fulfill their Visions is very worthwhile. Everything you learn will further help you identify how you can best leverage whatever your Unique Strengths are in any given moment in order to continue pursuing your Vision with confidence.

Lessons have a way of repeating themselves until we learn what we are supposed to learn, and can identify the Steps necessary to move forward toward our Vision and through a Transformative time. As humans, we are wired to learn and grow...constantly. But we are also unique, so we will learn lessons in our own unique fashion and we will apply them toward our Vision in our own unique ways.

EXERCISE
APPRECIATING THE MOMENT

This exercise is an opportunity to be mindful of how moments may have an impact on helping you achieve your Vision. The more you recognize that life is a series of moments, the more you gain appreciation for each moment.

STEP 1: Over the course of the next few days, pay attention to moments. How you wake up, which foot you put on the floor first, who you pass on the street, who you say "hi" to, etc... As you experience new moments be aware of the feelings coming forward, but pause and question them. Try not to judge yourself, or your feelings or thoughts, just register the moments and ask yourself what the source of these feelings is as you experience new moments.

STEP 2: At the end of each day, write down at least ten new moments you experienced, what they were, what you felt or thought, where you think the feelings were coming from and how the moment might have an impact on your Vision. What did you learn about yourself in each moment?

"Leadership is the capacity to translate vision into reality."

~ Warren Bennis

Chapter Thirteen

LEADERSHIP AND CONFIDENCE

Being Your Own Leader

WHAT MAKES A GOOD LEADER?

To be a good leader, you must be personally accountable for your choices and able to manage your fears while pursuing your Vision. You must also have the ability to inspire others to help you go after your Vision. Leadership means that you are able to challenge yourself to take the next Step toward the Goals that will put you on the path to realizing your Vision. In the face of an unexpected Transformative Moment, being a leader means that you have the courage to revisit and reevaluate your Unique Strengths, reconfirm or recreate your Vision, Goals and Steps, and go within to reexamine your motivations and fears. Leadership is having the faith in yourself to believe that your Vision is possible.

There are many skills and attributes that make up a good leader, but in simple terms, I define the common traits as follows:

1. **Ability to Process Information**—You learn and understand new information by really paying attention to the "moment." When your Vision is clear, it allows you to see things and identify opportunities that you might have missed otherwise. You are able to gather more useful information in order to make better choices that can help you in the pursuit of your Vision. Identifying and processing the information that is important in the pursuit of your Vision is simply easier when your Vision is clear.
2. **Ability to Organize Information**—Because you have outlined your Vision in bullet points, and written out the Goals and Steps you want to take, you know how to use the information you receive and can discern whether it will be helpful to you on your path toward the realization of your Vision.
3. **Ability to Prioritize Information**—You are able to identify what is most important and organize Steps to address it. If you find that you need to rearrange your Steps and take another Step first, you have the confidence to alter course due to the clarity that this prioritized information has provided you.

4. **Ability to Enroll Others**—You have a heightened degree of emotional intelligence and the ability to connect with and inspire others. You know that none of us can achieve our Vision alone, and that our Unique Strengths will only take us so far before we need to rely on the Unique Strengths of others. A leader understands this and is willing to do the research required to find partners, mentors and patrons. A leader also takes the time to understand and enroll him or herself into the Vision of others to create a win-win scenario.

5. **Ability to Communicate a Vision**—You are able to communicate a Vision to others the way they need the Vision to be communicated. You have done the exercises in this book and can clearly articulate your Vision, your Goals and the Steps you need to take to achieve your Vision. You understand that communicating your Vision is the quickest way to paint this picture for others. You also understand that while most people want to help, they don't always know how they can help. Communicating your Vision will allow others to add input that will help you in clarifying the next Steps you need to take.

6. **Ability to Protect Your Confidence**—This starts with believing that you will not fail in the pursuit of your Vision. You get that you will encounter roadblocks and obstacles, but your commitment to achieving your Vision is steadfast. As you reach milestones and accomplish Steps along the way, you find that your confidence grows and your belief in your ability to actually achieve your Vision grows stronger and stronger.

Following the process outlined in this book will help you to position yourself as the leader in YOUR life.

Leadership and Confidence

There is a difference between IQ (intellectual intelligence) and EQ (emotional intelligence). To lead with confidence, you need both. We develop IQ by reading, researching, traveling, exploring, investigating, and generally being willing to expand our minds in pursuit of knowledge about the world we live in and the people we live with. We can only develop EQ by taking the time to ask questions, listen, learn, and understand other people, their fears, motivations, and passions.

The "Platinum Rule" introduced in Chapter Six is a powerful tool for developing EQ, because it helps you see how another person needs to be treated or communicated with in order for them to genuinely understand what you are asking for or sharing. When we can see the world through another person's eyes, when we empathize with them, we are then able to truly connect with them.

Early in my career, I was introduced to the concept that there are four basic attitudes you will notice in people when you are trying to connect with them or lead them. This applies to any kind of relationship, personal or professional.

- **Acceptance**—They will follow you.
- **Indifference**—They see no perceived value in following you.
- **Skepticism**—They question whether you are worth following.
- **Objection**—There is some misunderstanding or perceived drawback in regards to following you.

Take the time to discern and understand the attitude you are faced with. Ask questions, understand the fear that is driving the motivation behind the attitudes of others.

If you encounter **Indifference**, you will need to ask questions to better understand your audience's Vision. It may be in conflict with your Vision. Usually, Indifference is the result of miscommunication. Ask questions to determine how what you're offering might be relevant to your audience.

If you encounter **Skepticism**, you may need to slow down, ask more questions and possibly offer up some evidence that you are sincere. You may need to explain the same thing multiple ways for someone to "get it."

Considering that no two people are alike, it only makes sense that no two people will see everything the same way. When you ask questions, you learn how you need to explain something so that the person you are speaking with can gain a clearer understanding of your Vision and needs.

If a person you are speaking with has an **Objection** to what you are offering, that person may have perceived some sort of drawback to being in collaboration with you. Again, you may need to ask more questions to gain more information and then rephrase your explanation in order to remove perceived drawbacks and create greater clarity.

When we take the time to handle the attitudes we are faced with, what we find is that we remove fears and we build confidence—confidence in ourselves as well as others. The number one trait you can build in others is the confidence to move forward.

I'M PROUD OF YOU

During Sammy's sophomore year in college, she took a class in marketing merchandising that spanned over two semesters. This class was responsible for putting on the annual Spring Fashion Show for the college. The school had invited top fashion experts from some of the largest and most prestigious companies from around the country. It was a BIG DEAL and very important to these students. It was their opportunity to show off their portfolio of work.

During our weekly chats, Sammy would talk about how it was progressing. She was working with the group of students who were responsible for organizing and marketing the show. She knew fashion, but was not a fashion designer herself. She was deeply involved in the logistics of pulling this event together, and was helping to design the website, tickets, pamphlets, and portfolio books. She was also responsible for managing the budget and hiring talent like photographers, videographers and others who were to play a role in the event.

Through those months of discussion, I was sometimes a sounding board for her, and a safe place for her to express her frustration. She was learning that it is sometimes a challenge to work with others. We'd talk things through, and I often found myself playing the role of teacher and cheerleader.

Early in my career, someone I respected shared with me that the number one thing you need to protect is your confidence. When we start thinking we can't do something, we usually don't even try. Sometimes there is a little voice in our head that is pushing us forward, but once we have lost all confidence, it is incredibly difficult to regain it. When we lose confidence, we often find ourselves stealing our own dreams.

"Sammy, I'm proud of you," I would say after every call no matter what she had shared with me. I was intentionally praising the process she was going through in the pursuit of her goals.

Saying, "Well done," or "I'm proud of you," or "Good work," or "Nice job," can be such a powerful and valuable ego boost. Praising the process and providing positive reinforcement can make a huge difference when you are helping someone reach their Goals toward achieving their Vision.

When you make it a habit of giving the gift of confidence to others, you will find that others will support you in return. Not everyone will of course, but more folks will support you than not. It becomes contagious, and it even becomes hard not to support someone who is supporting you. If you want to surround yourself with cheerleaders who will provide you with the positive support you need to protect your confidence, and the support necessary to achieve your Vision and navigate your Transformative Moments, start by being the cheerleader for others.

EXERCISE
LEADERSHIP AND CONFIDENCE

STEP 1: Go back and read over all of the positive responses you received from the people you asked to tell you what they think your Unique Strengths are. This will reinforce your confidence.

STEP 2: Ask three or more new people to write you an email telling you what they see as your Unique Strengths. This will further increase your confidence. Respond to these emails and let each person know what you think his or her Unique Strength is. This will help you expand your network of those people with whom you can start sharing your Vision.

STEP 3: After you have read the new emails and reviewed the old emails, take a moment to feel proud of yourself!

STEP 4: Pay close attention to the next five conversations you have with different people when you are trying to share an idea (or your Vision) with them. Determine whether any of the four Attitudes showed up in the conversations.

- **Acceptance**—They will follow you.
- **Indifference**—They see no perceived value in following you.

- **Skepticism**—They question whether you are worth following.
- **Objection**—There is some misunderstanding or perceived drawback in regards to following you.

After each conversation, ask yourself, "Which attitude did I encounter, and how could I have best addressed it?" Keep practicing this step in future conversations to enhance your EQ (Emotional Intelligence) and ability to communicate, both of which you will need to effectively enroll others in the pursuit of your Vision.

"Peace cannot be kept by force;

it can only be achieved by understanding."

~ Albert Einstein

CHAPTER FOURTEEN

GRATITUDE AND PEACE

Saying Thank You

GRATEFUL FOR A RAINY DAY

It was Saturday morning and I was supposed to play golf, but it was pouring rain outside, and it was not the kind of rain that just drizzles for a bit and then goes away. Disappointed, I texted my friends: "I'm out for golf. It's pouring." I laid in bed listening to the rain hit the roof, and decided that I didn't need to rush to get up. All my plans had changed, it was now going to be an inside day.

I found myself thinking about all the things I could get done that I'd been putting off for a long time. I could fix the leaky faucet and send out the invitations for my mother's 75th birthday party. I could do my laundry, and clean out the basement I'd been neglecting for about a year. I could get my grocery shopping done, and backup my computer, and replace the ink in my printer. I could also meet a friend for lunch, and then rent some movies and just relax later that night.

I found a new enthusiasm and sense of gratitude for what I was going to get done. I loved to golf, but the rain had made it very easy for me to change plans and find new opportunities. I got out of bed and went to work. In the process, I found all sorts of other little things I could accomplish that day. With each item that was taken care of I felt a sense of achievement and a sense of gratitude. That feeling of gratitude kept growing and spurring me on. I worked for about six hours and probably accomplished about twenty little things.

When I was thirteen and a baseball game got rained out, I hated it. As an adult, I have learned to practice gratitude. I have learned to appreciate each day for what it is and the little "wins" I experience when I take on the day with a sense of gratitude. How we choose to wake up in the morning is how our day will go. When we practice gratitude, we find that we start the day full of optimism and anticipation.

Practicing Gratitude

When Betsy first identified her Unique Strengths, developed her Vision, set Goals and Steps, and made a list of the people she could enroll in her Vision, she felt a bit unsure about how it was all going to play out. The fact is that none of us can know exactly how our lives will play out. The only thing we can be sure of is whether we are taking Steps in a direction that we believe will lead us toward our Vision.

Betsy wrote down her twenty Vision bullet points and then went to work connecting with those people who could help her take the Steps she needed to take in order to move forward. I recall following up with Betsy about once a week to check in on her progress. She would start every conversation by telling me about the positive encounters she'd had during the week.

She expressed gratitude for each encounter she'd had and each Step she took. Her confidence was growing and her appreciation for the journey was beginning to mature. She related stories about even the smallest wins she was accomplishing and how they might help her reach her Vision. Each week her stories grew and she had more to share.

She would also encounter setbacks, but as she shared stories of setbacks, she would also recount what she'd learned from the experience. She was practicing gratitude and she was finding something positive in just about every event and moment in her life. She was taking the time to say "thank you" for whatever it was she was experiencing.

Over the next couple of years, as Betsy put this practice of gratitude to work, the opportunities she needed to achieve her Goals and ultimately her Vision started to come into her life at a faster pace than she'd ever experienced before. She would be grateful for one thing she accomplished, and almost like magic, a second thing would be accomplished and knocked off her Vision list.

In less than two years, Betsy had accomplished eighteen of her twenty Vision bullet points! In addition, as Betsy practiced the Art of Gratitude, she found that she was becoming more confident, and much happier. She experienced a deep sense of peace within and ever increasing motivation to follow through on the Steps she needed to take to reach her Goals.

How Do I Show Gratitude?

People ask me, "How do I show gratitude?" It starts with intentionally saying "thank you" as often as you can in a day, and in every moment possible. Say "thank you" to the clerk who sells you a bottle of water. Say "thank you" to your children for giving you a morning hug. Say "thank you" because the parking space right in front of the doors to the mall is open. Say "thank you" to yourself for that $20 dollar lunch you just treated yourself to. Say "thank you" for having a pair of shoes to put on.

Gratitude is appreciating the whole journey. It's taking a moment to say "thank you" to the people who come into our lives, "thank you" for the moments, gifts, opportunities, lessons learned, and laughs. It's a small world with many like-minded people. They are all around us. They are on the same journey. At the end of the day, they too want to feel safe, be happy, and have sense of purpose. Be grateful that you are not on this journey alone. You've been given this life to live. Make the most of it. Be grateful. Practice acts of gratitude. Tell others "thank you." Give them a hug.

The more you focus on feeling grateful for those who have come into your life, in addition to the moments and experiences that fill your life, the more others feel the gratitude and want to be a part of your energy. The more opportunity you have to share your Vision and enroll others, the more quickly you will be able to accomplish your Vision. People will connect you to events, moments, and experiences in life. Without another person helping you, it's almost impossible to connect with those things you desire in your life. The more you show gratitude, the more of everything you receive in return.

When we practice expressing our gratitude on a daily basis we can feel our demeanor change. We can feel the energy it is giving us when we come from an attitude of true gratitude. Get started by saying "thank you." When you make this a habit, you will also find that you spend less time judging and more time appreciating moments and people for what they have to offer.

EXERCISE
GRATITUDE

My father died on Memorial Day weekend some years ago. I was deeply grateful that I was able to get to Montana to spend his last twenty-four hours with him. I was grateful that he didn't have a lot of pain and suffering, and I was grateful for being able to watch his transition from life to death. It may sound odd that I was grateful for experiencing that moment, but in the process of doing so, I gained a much deeper clarity about the purpose of my own life.

I felt a greater sense of commitment to my Vision, and a greater commitment to get things like this book done. The clarity of seeing that it all physically comes to an end, created a feeling of gratitude within for still having the physical abilities to achieve my personal Vision. When you are consciously practicing gratitude, you take every moment as an opportunity to learn something. And, conversely, if you recognize that every moment is a learning opportunity, you are able to be grateful for each of those moments.

STEP 1: Write down ten things you are grateful for right now.

STEP 2: In the next three days say "thank you" with intention a hundred times (thirty-three times per day). It might be to the barista at a coffee shop, a classmate who picks up a pencil for you, a teacher who shares something interesting, or a coworker who shares some knowledge with you.

STEP 3: Write down changes you notice in your attitude and perceptions from practicing gratitude.

"It's kind of fun to do the impossible."

~ Walt Disney

Epilogue

DREAM BIG!

Early on in the development of Project OTY, someone said to me that what I was describing as my Vision was like wanting to live in a world with rainbows and unicorns.

My response was, "What would be so bad about that?"

His reply was, "It's not possible..."

I countered with, "That's what you've been led to believe. Why can't everyone live a safe, happy and fulfilling life?"

The information in this book has been learned over a lifetime. The order of the lessons seems to be the most efficient path for creating YOUR world and a life YOU are passionate about living. I've seen this process change lives. I've seen people achieve things they never imagined possible. I know that when I have applied the exercises and lessons outlined in this book, they have allowed me to Transform with Confidence every time.

I can only imagine the impact this book and Project OTY would have if the next couple of generations of young people embrace the concepts and do the exercises I've presented. We'd be better equipped to solve societal issues that affect all of us. We'd have the tools to create a stronger economy that benefits everyone. We'd be able to shift entrenched belief systems and prejudices that don't support growth, health, and happiness. I believe it's possible.

If you feel inspired to learn more about Project OTY, we're excited to connect with you. If you're inspired to introduce others to Project OTY, we're excited to connect with them. In fact, building a community is what Project OTY is all about. Imagine if you and your spouse, or you and your partner, or you and your community really understood each other's Visions. Those around you could help you be personally accountable in the pursuit of your Vision, and collectively, you and your spouse, partner or community could achieve more than you ever thought possible.

Please visit ProjectOTY.com.

I wish you the best in your continued journey.
Dream Big!

WHO'S JEFF OTIS?

I'm a dad, a business leader, a coach, a mentor and a friend to many. I grew up in a loving family, participated in athletics and was fortunate to be surrounded by strong mentors, coaches and peers.

I spent 15 years in the employment staffing industry building sales and service teams around the country. I interviewed 1,000's of applicants and had over 10,000 employees reporting to me directly or indirectly over the years. It all added up to lots of people time. I was very fortunate that the company I worked for spent a considerable amount of its revenues on training in the areas of sales, self-awareness, leadership and personal growth.

I then spent 11 years working in the online marketing, messaging and advertising world. I helped lead two companies to being ranked an Inc 5000 Fastest Growing Private Company for 9 of those years. All 3 companies were voted a Best Company to Work For. All 3 were full of great leaders, managers and staff.

In the process, I've spoken to well over 100,000 business leaders of all types from around the country working in just about every industry imaginable. I've spent considerable time studying human behavior, neuroscience and the concepts of neuromarketing.

And... I've tried to capture the best of the best of what I've learned in this book to share and inspire a generation or two. Maybe more?

Enjoy the Book. Create Your World.

Transform with Confidence!

Thank you!
Jeff

www.ingramcontent.com/pod-product-compliance
Lightning Source LLC
Chambersburg PA
CBHW071917290426
44110CB00013B/1388